ISSUES IN SOCIOLOGY
Edited by Robert G. Burgess

The Media

Beverley Skeggs
Lecturer in Educational Studies, University of York

John Mundy
Senior Lecturer in Media, North Cheshire College
Lecturer in Film Studies, University of Manchester

Nelson

Thomas Nelson and Sons Ltd
Nelson House Mayfield Road
Walton-on-Thames Surrey
KT12 5PL UK

51 York Place
Edinburgh
EH1 3JD UK

Thomas Nelson (Hong Kong) Ltd
Toppan Building 10/F
22A Westlands Road
Quarry Bay Hong Kong

Thomas Nelson Australia
102 Dodds Street
South Melbourne
Vic 3205 Australia

Nelson Canada
1120 Birchmount Road
Scarborough Ontario
M1K 5G4 Canada

13313290

©1992 Beverley Skeggs and John Mundy

First published by Thomas Nelson and Sons Ltd 1992

ISBN 0–17–4384467
NPN 9 8 7 6 5 4 3 2

Printed in Hong Kong

Contents

For Mum and Dad

For Karen

Series Editor's Preface

The aim of the *Issues in Sociology* series is to provide easy access to debates and controversies in different fields of study within sociology. In particular, the series is designed for students who are beginning sociology as part of sixth form study or in further education, or in adult and continuing education classes.

The books in the series are written by authors who have wide experience of research and teaching in a special field of study where they have been directly involved in key debates. In this way, they are able to communicate the richness of the subject to the student. At the beginning of each volume, an introductory essay presents an outline of the field where key issues, problems and debates are identified. In subsequent chapters, the student is provided with commentaries, extracts, questions for discussion, essays and guides to further reading. The result is a work book that can be used by the individual student or by teachers working with small groups or a whole class.

Altogether the material in each volume seeks to convey the way in which sociological research involves a knowledge of theory and method as well as a detailed understanding of an area of study.

This volume on the media provides a basic introduction to this area for students of sociology and those engaged in the study of communication. The authors have provided a useful guide to the key issues and debates on the media and have presented a series of stimulating questions for further discussion by students.

Robert G. Burgess
University of Warwick

Acknowledgements

Beverley would like to thank her parents for all the support and sustenance they have provided, especially her mother, Doreen, for all the filing and her father, Ken, for the typing. Gratitude and appreciation are also due to Nickie Witham, Val Atkinson, Pat Kirkham, Erica Stratta, Amos Zamorski, Mark Jancovich and Mica Nava for the sharpening up of arguments and for all their support.

The authors and publishers wish to thank the following who have kindly given permission for the use of copyright material:

The authors and publishers wish to acknowledge the following photographic source: Universal Pictorial Press, p. 26.
Marion Boyars Publishers Ltd. for material from *Decoding Advertisements: Idealogy and Meaning in Advertising* by Judith Williamson, 1978; British Film Institute for material from *The Broadcasting Debate: The Neglected Audience* eds. Tana Wollen and Janet Willis, 1990, pp. 1–2; Campaign for Press and Broadcasting Freedom for material from 'Media in the dock', *Free Press*, May/ June 1990; Guardian News Service Ltd. for material from 4.2.89 and 15.1.90 issues of *The Guardian*; HarperCollins Publishers for material from 'The Political Effects of Television' by Jay. G. Blumler in *The Effects of Television* ed. J. Halloran, Panther Books, 1970; and *Pictures of Human Sexuality* by J. Root, Pandora Press, 1984; The Controller of Her Majesty's Stationery Office for material from *Broadcasting in the United Kingdom 1981* and *Cm 517: Broadcasting in the 90's, Competition, Choice and Quality*; Manchester University Press for material from *The End of Century Party: Youth and Pop Towards 2000* by S. Redhead, 1990; New Left Review for material from 'Base and Superstructure in Marxist Cultural Theory' by R. Williams, *New Left Review*, 82, Dec. 1973; Newspaper Publishing PLC for 'Commons united in opposition to media empires', *The Independent*, 20.5.89; New Statesman and Society for 'Technological Thrills' by M. Davidson, *NS & S*, 12.5.89 and 'Taking Liberties' by J. Jenkins, *NS & S*, 17.8.90; Routledge for material from *Making Sense of the Media* by J. Hartley, H. Goulden and T. Sullivan, Comedia, 1985; 'The Political Economy of Culture' by S. Jhally in *Cultural Politics in Contemporary America* eds I. Angus and S. Jhally, Routledge, 1989; 'Negotiation of control in media organizations and occupations' in *Culture, Society and the Media* eds M. Gurevitch, T. Bennett, J. Curran and J. Woollacott, Routledge, 1988; *Power Without Responsibility: The Press and Broadcasting in Britain*, by J. Curran and J. Seaton, 3rd. ed. 1988, Routledge; and 'Changing Paradigms in Audience Studies' in *Remote Control: Television Audiences and Cultural Power* eds Selter et al., Routledge, 1989; Sage Publications Ltd. for material from 'Pierre Bourdieu and the Sociology of Culture: An Introduction' by N. Garnham and R. Williams in *Capitalism and Communication: Global Culture and the Economics of Information* ed. N. Garnham, 1990; *Mass Communication Theory: An Introduction* by D. McQuail, 2nd ed. 1987; and 'The politics of polysemy: television news, everyday consciousness and political action' by K. B. Jensen, *Media, Culture and Society*, Vol. 12, 1990; Philip Schlesinger for material from *Putting 'Reality' Together*, 2nd ed. Constable, 1987; Screen material from 'Don't Look Now' by R. Dyer, *Screen*, Vol. 23, 3/4, 1983; and 'The Impact of Technological and Political Change on the Labour Force in British Television' by C. Sparks, *Screen*, Vol. 30, 1/2, 1989; The University of Birmingham and the author for 'Television and 'The North'', Working Paper in Cultural Studies, by R. Adams, 1985, Centre for Contemporary Cultural Studies; and 'Life's more fun with your number one Sun: Interviews with some *Sun* readers', Stencilled Occasional Paper, No. 85 by M. Pursehouse, 1987, Centre for Contemporary Cultural Studies; Verso for material from *Reading the Romance* by J. Radway, 1987; and Introduction from *Female Spectators: Looking at Film and Television* by E. D. Pribram, 1988

Every effort has been made to trace all the copyright holders, but if any have been inadvertently overlooked the publishers will be pleased to make the necessary arrangement at the first opportunity.

Introduction

Together with key social institutions, such as the family and education, the mass media have come to be regarded as crucial elements in social organisation. Listening to the radio, playing records, tapes and compact discs, going to the cinema, reading newspapers, comics and magazines, watching television and video cassettes are central activities, not just in terms of the time and money spent on them and their importance as leisure activities, but also because they are the prime site through which human beings, as active social participants construct meanings, beliefs and values.

When a popular national daily newspaper sells over four million copies and is read by over 11 million readers a day; when a television soap opera commands a regular audience of 16 million; when over 350 million video cassette rental films are watched by 1050 million viewers in a year; and when Radio One's Top 40 programme attracts nearly five million listeners every Sunday evening, it seems clear that media commodities and their regular consumption form an important aspect of all our daily lives.

Recent statistics show that the 'average' person in Britain watches 26 hours of television a week. Looked at purely from this perspective of individual consumption of the media, it is obvious that the media assume a social significance which demands examination and analysis.

But, of course, systematic study of the media involves confronting issues which are much more extensive and important than this. What we argue in this book is that the mass media are significant for a number of reasons:

1. As an industry which selects and employs a wide range of people for a variety of jobs, and which produces goods for consumption.
2. As a powerful institution in its own right, with its own distinctive ways of operating, but one which also interacts with a range of other social institutions.
3. As a mechanism through which power and control are exercised in society, a mechanism which is itself a site for conflict

over ownership, control and access.

4. As a prime site through which social meanings and our sense of reality are constructed and challenged, through the ideologically informed representation of ideas, issues and events.

5. As an arena for pleasure and consumption, through which human beings define and express their sense of place within the social formation.

Of course, although we argue that an understanding of the mass media is important if we want to understand our contemporary society, we should not lose sight of the basic notion that, fundamentally, all societies are structured by differences of power which exist between groups. In all societies, these differences find expression in conflicts, tensions and struggles, some of which are more visible and obvious than others. What makes the media so important is that they have become one of the most significant social arenas in which these conflicts and tensions, and the varying ideological assumptions which underpin them, find expression.

Yet, even though most sociologists would probably agree that the mass media are an important aspect of contemporary society, it would be wrong to ignore the wide and differing range of theories which exist about the media and their significance. Whenever we read, see or hear commentaries on the media, whether they are considering the relationship of the media to the state, organisational and technological aspects of the media institutions, or the conditions in which media texts are circulated and consumed, we are faced with views which are inconsistent and often deeply contradictory. Arguably, these opposing viewpoints result, not just from different interpretations of available evidence, but from the much more fundamental divisions of interest and value which operate in society. Debates about newspaper ownership and control, or about the changing structure of broadcasting are important in themselves, but they are also important for what they reveal about issues of power, value and ideology which permeate the social structure.

One measure of the growing importance of the mass media in societies such as ours is the rapid expansion in the number of books, magazines and journals which attempt to describe and perhaps explain ways in which the media have become significant to us. Some of these are concerned to look at ways in which industrial and organisational structures influence and shape programmes or 'texts'. Others are concerned with the distribution and consumption of media products and their effects on audiences who read, see and listen to them. Some examine ways in which the media are affected by technological development, whilst others focus on the actual content of media products to see how they attempt to construct particular meanings according to structured sets of cultural conventions.

In this book, we concentrate on those issues that are the most significant from a sociological perspective. Beginning with the key issue of the relationship between the state and the media, we concentrate on the structures and patterns of ownership and control of the media, and the often contradictory positions which result from this complex relationship. In doing this, we will be concerned with fundamental questions about the exercise of power in society.

Turning our attention to the media as institution, we explore ways in which institutional structures, together with political, social and ideological pressures, affect the ways in which those working within the media carry out their jobs. Although media workers may see themselves as professionals, responsible to the public at large, the extent to which they have a free hand in exercising this general responsibility is constrained by the structures and organisations they work for. By examining issues of professionalism, independence and accountability, we raise questions about ways in which power is exercised in society, and introduce the debate about whether the media represent a means for maintaining social order and consensus, or for possible social change.

Following this, we examine the key role played by the mass media in the social construction of reality. The media occupy a space between our everyday experiences and the meaning that we make of them, through the process of mediation. Arguing that our access to 'reality' comes essentially from its media representations, we examine the different theoretical perspectives, and their ideological determinants, which have been applied to this process of mediation. By looking at specific representations of issues such as gender and class within particular media forms, we raise questions about the relationship between reality, representation and ideology.

Any study of the mass media makes a basic assumption that they have an influence and effect upon us. Yet, as we shall see, not only are there conflicting views about the concept of 'audience', there is widespread disagreement about just what these influences and effects are, and how they work. Traditionally, much of the debate has centred around the concept of how the media amplifies and exaggerates issues, and how it is involved in constructing the agenda of social issues that we come to consider as important. However, recent research suggests alternative – or at least additional – models which need consideration. The question of what we do with the media is arguably as important as the question of what the media do to us.

Finally, we look at ways in which new technology and its attendant changes are influencing media production and consumption. For many, new technologies are seen as offering exciting challenges to existing structures, institutions and attitudes. Others see the utilisation of new technology as being the means by which the perpetuation and reinforcement of established patterns of ownership and control, and of dominant ideologies, can be maintained.

In providing the commentary and extracts which follow, we hope to encourage responses to some basic, but essential, questions about the mass media and their sociological significance. For McQuail (1987), the basic questions to be answered are:

1. Who controls the media and in whose interest?
2. Who has access to the media and on what terms?
3. Whose version of the world (social reality) is presented?
4. How effective are the media in achieving their chosen ends?

There are a number of underlying questions and concerns which form the basis for this book. Do the media only represent the interests of those with the money and the power to have their opinions expressed? To what extent does government use the media to control oppositional views and therefore win support for its own policies? Will those social groups without access to power ever have access to an equality of representation? Is it inevitable that people will always construct their own personal feelings and experiences through the ideological framework constructed for them by the media? To what extent will the growth of ever more powerful transnational companies owning the media affect national culture?

As the extracts suggest, the answers to these questions depend upon the theoretical perspectives which are brought to bear on them. An understanding and appreciation of that will, we hope, lead to an understanding of the nature of sociological enquiry itself.

Introductory Reading

Frank Allaun (1989) *Spreading The News*, Spokesman Press. A partial and heartfelt analysis of contemporary media, with an emphasis on newspapers.

M. Alvarado, R. Gutch and T. Wollen (1987) *Learning The Media: An Introduction to Media Teaching*, Macmillan. Although written primarily with teachers in mind, this is an extremely useful overview of key issues in Media Studies.

David Barrett (1986) *Media Sociology*, Tavistock. A good introduction to the study of the media from a sociological perspective.

B. Dutton and J. Mundy (1989) *Media Studies: An Introduction*, Longmans. A bright and breezy, but very basic, introduction to studying the media, useful only to those with little or no prior knowledge.

John Fiske (1988) *Introduction To Communication Studies*, Routledge. An excellent introduction to communication theory and its relevance in understanding the mass media.

Peter Golding (1974) *The Mass Media*, Longman. A very lucid introduction, but inevitably somewhat dated now.

J. Hartley, H. Goulden and T. O'Sullivan (1985) *Making Sense of the Media*, Comedia. As the title suggests, a series of booklets which examines how we make sense of the media as individual text, as popular culture, and as institution.

Stuart Hood (1987) *On Television*, 3rd edn, Pluto Press. An excellent introductory account of the political, economic and cultural context of British television.

Denis McQuail (1987) *Mass Communication Theory: An Introduction*, 2nd edn, Sage. An excellent, though at times detailed and exhaustive textbook on the sociology of the mass media.

Vincent Porter (1988) *On Cinema*, Pluto Press. A companion volume to Hood, equally useful.

Jeremy Tunstall (1983) *The Media in Britain*, Constable. Penetrating and informative introduction to the sociology of the media.

1 | Ownership and control

The media are one of the main sites for the production and circulation of ideas. The way we think about ourselves, others, issues and events is often related to the interpretive frameworks provided by the media. This chapter will examine how and why certain ideas come to be circulated and others excluded. It will examine the power relationships behind the production of ideas, and it will ask 'in whose interests' are certain ideas put forward. If everybody in society had access to expressing themselves within the media, we would not be addressing these problems. However, as this chapter will demonstrate, only certain groups have access to, and power over, media output.

In an attempt to explore the role and influence of economic concerns Murdock and Golding (1973) argue that the media are first and foremost industrial and commercial organisations which produce and distribute commodities. The media companies are locked into the wider economic situation, firstly through reciprocal investments and shareholdings and interlocking directorships with other large industrial concerns, and secondly, through advertising.

However, what distinguishes the media from other economic sectors is that they are involved in the production, circulation and distribution of ideas. Because our contact with media products is in the sphere of ideas, we often forget that these ideas are the product of an industrial process. Murdock and Golding distinguish the forms of economic development which apply to the media as much as any other industries within capitalism.

1. *From differentiation to concentration*, the process whereby a large number of owners is reduced, through mergers and acquisitions, to a small number, leading to concentration of ownership. In Britain today, three large corporations account for 75 per cent of the national circulation of daily newspapers.
2. *Consolidation and diversification*, in which companies expand their interests across a broad range of media and other business activities. Reed International, for example, have extensive interests in a range of activities such as DIY and building products, as well as extensive publishing interests.

3. *Integration*, or the process by which companies acquire other media interests through mergers and takeovers. Lonrho, for example, has interests in newspapers and commercial television.
4. *Internationalisation*, whereby companies extend their interests beyond the limitations of national boundaries into global markets. Some transnational companies (TNCs), such as IBM, have a presence in as many as 130 countries.

We can understand some of these points by looking at the extensive interests of the transnational News Corporation, owned by Rupert Murdoch, which has media and other commercial interests in Britain, the United States, Australia and many other countries. In 1989 the main holdings of News Corporation were:

Main British press interests	*Selected other media interests*	*Selected non-media interests*
The Sun	Sky Channel (4)	Ansett Transport
News of the World	Collins (Fontana)	Santos (natural gas)
The Times	Channel 10 Sydney	News-Eagle (oil)
The Sunday Times	*Herald* and *Weekly*	Snodland Fibres
Today	Times group (Aust.)	Whitefriars
	Metromedia (US)	Investment
	20th Century Fox	

It is clear from this that the economic determinants are crucial in understanding media ownership and control. However, descriptions of ownership patterns do not tell us how the owners use their influence and control within the realm of ideas. In fact, the relationship between ownership and control is more complex. We have to take into account that control is not always exercised directly, nor does the economic state of the media organisations have an obvious and immediate effect on their output. Moreover, state intervention and regulation can add a further complicating dimension. For instance, we need to explain the existence of media activities such as cinema and publishing which, far from providing instant profits, can sometimes operate with long-term financial losses. Equally, we have to take into account state operated media which are financed wholly or in part by public subscription or taxation.

Reference

G. Murdock and P. Golding (1973) 'For a political economy of mass communications', in R. Miliband and J. Savile (eds) *The Socialist Register 1973*, Merlin Press.

☐ Freedom of the Press?

Liberal theorists of the media would argue that ownership is not a significant factor in understanding how ideas come to be produced and circulated, since they believe, for example, that everybody is free to own and run a newspaper. This 'common-sense' view of Britain's press is quite widely held by many practising journalists, as the following extract illustrates.

Reading 1

Britain has a free press. There is no censor and no licensing, and anyone can publish a newspaper provided he or she does not break the law in doing so. The press is in private hands. There is no Government controlled newspaper, no Government shareholding in a newspaper, and the press gets no form of Government help other than the exemption of VAT [value added tax]. The sessions of Parliament are open to the press and the workings of the Government are reported and commented on, as are the workings of all other public institutions.

The freedom of the press is not inscribed upon tablets of stone as it is in the American constitution; it exists by consensus, and the freedom British newspapers enjoy and for which journalists fought over the centuries has to be guarded by editors, by political parties and by the people who care about these matters. It is guarded, above all by the Press Council, the voluntary regulating body for the industry, in whose constitution this duty is spelt out . . .

Operating thus freely, British newspapers offer a wide spectrum of political and social views. Though there is only one party-aligned daily, the Communist *Morning Star*, the national press presents political standpoints ranging from the solid Right to the extreme Left (though with a bias in volume circulation to the Right). National newspapers also serve a variety of social groups. There are also daily and weekly newspapers and magazines published in support of religions, political fringe groups, trade unions, the entertainment industry, homosexuals, even the brewing and licensing trade. And there are local papers of every kind, including free sheets. Anyone who can find the money – and the readers – can start a newspaper.

Source

F. W. Hodgson (1984) *Modern Newspaper Practice*, Heinemann, pp. 168–9.

Questions

1. What, according to Hodgson, are the main safeguards of British press freedom?
2. Are there any remarks of Hodgson's which might lead you to question his assurance that the British press represents a wide spectrum of political and social opinion?
3. Can you think of recent examples which may or may not support Hodgson's view that anyone can start a newspaper?

☐ The 'Base/Superstructure' Model

Rather than believing that we have equal access to ownership, Marxist theorists argue that because of the unequal distribution of wealth in society, only certain groups will have access to ownership, and that in order to maintain their position at the top of the social and economic stratification they will use the media to consolidate their power and wealth.

Reading 2

What is at stake between these opposing perspectives is the relationship between the economic base and the ideological super-structure. The starting point for understanding the relationship between economy and culture is the work of Karl Marx. Marx wrote that there is a very close connection between the control of material wealth and the control of ideas and culture, for the ruling class is able to dictate (because of their control of the 'means of mental production' such as the media) the context in which people think about their daily lives. Consequently, what people accept as 'natural' and 'self-evident' is exactly what should become problematic and in need of explanation from a critical standpoint. It is characteristic of Marxist thought to place the conscious expressions of social actors within the whole social complex in which those expressions occur. This theoretical framework has generally been described under what is called the 'base/superstructure' model. Briefly, this means that the economic base conditions the contents of the superstructure of ideas and beliefs in everyday life.

Source

I. Angus and S. Jhally (eds) (1989) 'Introduction', *Cultural Politics in Contemporary America*, Routledge, pp. 12–13.

Questions

1. Why do you think that the authors believe that there is a very close relationship between the control of wealth and the control of ideas?
2. (a) Why are the authors interested in questioning what we take for 'natural' and 'self-evident'?
   (b) Is this questioning role important for a sociologist? Give reasons for your answer.
3. Using examples, explain how the 'base/superstructure' model operates within the media industry.

□ Legitimating Control

An understanding of the relationship between material production and the circulation of ideas forms the basis of more sophisticated attempts which try to understand the relationship between the owners of the media and the control that they are able to exercise. The next reading suggests that the owners deliberately use the media to maintain their profit-making interests; it is called the 'consciousness industry' approach.

Reading 3

For societies, such as capitalism, that are characterised by a wide disparity in the distribution of wealth and power, one of the major concerns is how a minority but dominant social class (capitalists) can maintain power over the vast majority of the population. There are two ways in which this reproduction can be accomplished. First, by sheer force . . . Second, through the consent of the dominated, by convincing the majority to identify and support the present system of rewards and power rather than opposing it, in fact to live their domination as freedom. In this the media are vital institutions that, far from providing a free marketplace of ideas, work to legitimate the existing distribution of power by controlling the context within which people think and define social problems and their possible solutions. In one very important variant of critical communications theory the function of the media and the cultural realm in general is to produce the appropriate consciousness in the majority of people to ensure the reproduction of what is essentially an exploitative system of social relations. Hans Enzenberger coined the phrase 'Consciousness Industry' to describe the media. The media here are literally an industry which attempts to produce a form of consciousness in the audience that benefits the class that controls the media and industry in general.

This control is achieved concretely by means of interlocking directorships, by persons who serve on the board of directors of multiple corporations, and thus can coordinate the interests they represent. These directors are responsible for hiring and firing people in important media posts. That is where their power rests, not on interference with reporters and editors at an everyday level. The implications for the cultural realm of such connections between the media and the economy are immense. Take the following example: the debate concerning the *arms race*. Many of the companies who benefit from huge defence contracts are intimately connected with the media. How is the debate going to be affected by that relationship? For example, General Electric [in the USA] is a major defence contractor for the government. GE (through its ownership of RCA) owns and operates the NBC [National Broad-casting Corporation]. Within this context how will the SDI (or 'Star Wars') debate be framed and structured on NBC? If SDI proceeds, General Electric will reap the rewards in billions of dollars! It is little wonder that serious and informed debate about the arms race is almost totally absent from television.

Source

S. Jhally (1989) 'The Political Economy of Culture', in I. Angus and S. Jhally (eds), *Cultural Politics in Contemporary America*, Routledge, pp. 67–9.

Questions

1. How do the minority with interests in capital win the consent of the majority of the population?
2. Why does Enzenberger describe the media as a 'Consciousness Industry'?
3. What is one of the main ways that control is exercised by those with powerful interests in the media?

☐ The Media as a Commodity

Whilst recognising that interlocking ownerships are likely to influence the framework for the debate of ideas, this is not necessarily an automatically determined process. The next extract develops this position by presenting the 'industrialisation of culture' perspective. Garnham (1986) argues that we have to move towards an understanding of the media which is premised upon historical materialism, because it is this which underlines the relationships, the forms and the content of the media. Arguably, the necessary condition for a capitalist social formation is the existence of a more or less universal domination of social relations by the exchange relation, i.e. a market economy. Garnham maintains that the social formation will not always be equally balanced and smooth-running, because the economy does not always determine all the other elements of the system. Rather, through a series of shifting relationships between the economic and other influences such as the state, the capitalist social formation follows an uneven and contradictory development.

Reading 4

The research perspective I have outlined, attempts to shift attention away from the conception of the media as Ideological State Apparatus and sees them first as economic entities ... When we buy a newspaper we participate simultaneously in an economic exchange, in subjection to or reaction against an ideological formation and often a quite specific act of political identification ... We also know that from the analysis of the development of the press that the nature of the political involvement is quite specifically

economically conditioned. Similarly, TV news is economically determined within commodity production in general, performs an ideological function and explicitly operates within politics, in terms of
balance, etc. . . . Indeed one of the key features of the mass media
within monopoly capitalism has been the exercise of political and
ideological domination through the economic . . . Because capital
controls the means of cultural production in the sense that the
production and exchange of cultural commodities become the
dominant forms of cultural relationship, it does not follow that these
cultural commodities will necessarily support, either in their explicit
content or in their mode of cultural appropriation, the dominant
ideology . . . There is then, no necessary coincidence between the
effects of the capitalist process proper and the ideological needs of
the dominant class.

Source

N. Garnham (1986) 'Contribution to a political economy of mass communications', in
R. Collins, J. Curran, N. Garnham, P. Scannell, P. Schlesinger and C. Sparks (eds),
Media, Culture and Society: a Critical Reader, pp. 18–21.

Questions

1. (a) What is a 'market economy'?
   (b) What does Garnham see as being the necessary condition for a
   market economy?
2. What processes does Garnham argue that we are engaged in when we
   buy a newspaper?
3. What are the differences between the 'industrialisation of culture' and
   the 'Consciousness Industry' (see Reading 3) perspectives?

□ Selling
   Us
   Water

The following reading gives an example of the other important
influences that can be brought to bear in the relationship between
the economic and the ideological, namely the role of the state. In
this example, the state is using the market of advertising to
circulate specific ideas and win support for its economic policies.
The £2.25 million spent on promoting the Government's proposals
for the National Health Service would be another example.

Reading 5

By their ads ye shall know them. Perhaps two of the most emblematic instances of what the past 10 years have wrought, are to be found in two recent commercials. The first is called *Sky to Tap* and the second is called *Toilet*. They each climax with a child, white male of about five years of age, having a drink of water. The first stretches his hand into the crystal cascade pouring from the kitchen tap, filling his glass with not-yet-privatised water. His innocent gesture is one that millions of us will see again and again over the next few weeks as the '10 water and sewage businesses in England and Wales' turn up the volume on their self-promotion. The first campaign will earn its promoters, the agency D'Arcy Masius Benton and Bowles, millions of pounds and a high commercial profile; while the second has already won for its creators a D & AD silver award. Advertising has always been adept at selling politics; today it has learnt how to buy consciences. People usually advertise only because they have to, and until recently the water authorities didn't have to. Now they present themselves as attractive to investors. Following the Water Authority Association's 'image building', the actual flotations will be the object of a DoE campaign costing an estimated £15–20 million. Both of these campaigns will rank the government alongside the year's largest, up with the perennial big spenders, like Kelloggs Corn Flakes and Pedigree Petfood. The DoE money will be drawn from a government budget which has risen fivefold in four years, and is now set to break the £100 million barrier, seriously challenging the gargantuan spenders Unilever and Proctor and Gamble as the UK's biggest patrons of advertising.

The privatising and corporate campaigns of the eighties have spawned a new breed of advertising epic, able to make boring facts hum with noumenal, folksy wonder. *Sky to Tap* is 90 seconds of just thrilling bravura, once again telling us how we live at the nexus of vast and impressive systems, of technology and commitment that literally make the mind spin, soar and swoop. What we have here is not so much an ad as such, as a corporate requiem mass for advertising itself . . . The whole effect is incantatory, an invocation of faith initiating us with fleeting glimpses of a purer, invisible world of power and grace. It is very baptismal. This is the apotheosis of advertising, language that literally brooks no dissent, that taps an irrational capacity for wonder, and drowns us in non-negotiable streams of consciousness.

Source

M. Davidson (1989) 'Technological Thrills', in *New Statesman and Society*, 12 May, p. 42.

Questions

1. Why does the government spend so much money on advertising?
2. How does the example of the selling of the water industry relate to Enzenberger's theories about the 'Consciousness Industry'?
3. How does the above extract relate to Garnham's 'industrialisation of culture' theories?

☐ Market Forces

The increasing attention and expenditure by the government on advertising provides us with an indication of the changes in the type of control that is being exercised in the media. Whilst it is difficult for a government in a 'democratic' country to be seen interfering with the media, it is far easier to exercise control through influence upon market forces. Recently, this move has been articulated through the language of 'consumer demand', an example of which was the Peacock Committee which was set up to examine the possibility of financing the BBC through advertising.

Reading 6

Our own conclusion is that British broadcasting should move towards a sophisticated market system based on consumer sovereignty. That is a system which recognizes that viewers and listeners are the best ultimate judge of their own interests, which they can best satisfy if they have an option of purchasing the broadcasting services they require from as many alternative sources of supply as possible. There will always be a need to supplement the direct consumer market by public finance for programmes of a public service kind ... supported by people in their capacity as citizens and voters but unlikely to be commercially self-supporting in the view of broadcasting entrepreneurs.

Source

Home Office (1986) *Report of the Committee on Financing the BBC*, HMSO, para. 592 (commonly referred to as the Peacock Report).

Questions

1. What do you understand by the concept of 'a sophisticated market system based on consumer sovereignty'?
2. Where are the 'alternative sources of supply' likely to come from and how could they be guaranteed to offer a plurality of social interests?
3. To what extent do you think that the call for 'public finance' implies a weakness in the model put forward by the Peacock Committee?

☐ Total Control

The 1988 Government White Paper, *Broadcasting in the '90s: Competition, Choice and Quality*, proposes legislation that appears to relinquish control from the state and put it into the hands of the media owners. These greater opportunities for cross-media ownership make questions about the relationship between ownership and control more important than ever.

Reading 7

The Commons yesterday united in concern at the risks to objective news reporting and competition when national newspaper proprietors become television magnates.

'Cross-control of the media is wrong in principle and creates a situation where mischief can take a hold', John Wheeler, Conservative chairman of the Commons Home Affairs Select Committee, warned during a backbench debate on broadcasting ... Cross-ownership could lead to distortion of fair competition and to a lack of objective reporting both of which were contrary to the public interest.

'Pressure might be applied directly to journalists to write favourably about their proprietor's television interests or to avoid covering embarrassing stories', he said.

'These developments may lead to newspaper readers being fed a partial view of events or to the mixing of editorial coverage with promotional material.'

Mr Wheeler told MP's the problem of editorial uniformity was compounded when newspaper editors were also senior television executives. He did not mention by name Andrew Neil, editor of the *Sunday Times* and executive chairman of Sky, but he said: 'These issues have been brought into focus with the launch of Sky Television, controlled by News International which already owns 35% of our national newspapers . . . It is no coincidence that among the quality newspapers only *The Times*, a Murdoch newspaper, publishes the schedules of Sky Television.'

Source

'Commons united in opposition to media empires', *The Independent*, 20.5.89.

Questions

1. What evidence does the extract provide to suggest that MPs are aware of the connection between the economic and ideological aspects of media ownership?
2. From this reading can you ascertain whose interests the government appears to be representing?
3. How does this reading contrast with the earlier reading about the selling of the water industry?

Further Questions

1. Examine the relationship between ownership, control and production of the mass media. (*AEB 1983*)
2. Assess the extent to which ownership of the mass media can influence the content of the mass media. (*AEB 1988*)
3. 'Control of the mass media is an important aspect of elite power.' Discuss (*AEB 1982*)
4. Compare and contrast Enzenberger's 'Consciousness Industry' theories with Garnham's 'industrialisation of culture' theories.
5. Do the interests of the state or government necessarily coincide with those who own the media?

Further Reading

M. Alvarado, R. Gutch and T. Wollen (1988) *Learning The Media*, Macmillan, pp. 39–90.

T. Bairstow (1986) *Fourth Rate Estate*, Comedia.

J. Curran, M. Gurevitch and J. Woollacott (eds), (1977) *Mass Communication and Society*, Edward Arnold/Open University.

J. Curran and J. Seaton (1988) *Power Without Responsibility*, Routledge, 3rd edn, parts I, II and III.

M. Hollingsworth (1986) *The Press and Political Dissent: A Question of Censorship*, Pluto Press, 1986.

Home Office (1988) *Broadcasting in the '90s: Competition, Choice and Quality*, HMSO.

Denis McQuail (ed.) (1976) *Sociology of Mass Communication*, Penguin, chapters 1, 2 and 5.

Denis McQuail (1987) *Mass Communications Theory: An Introduction*, Sage, 2nd edn, 1987, especially chapters 1, 3 and 4.

2 | Media institutions

We have seen that issues associated with the ownership and control of the media can only really be understood within a transnational context, since it is the workings of international capital which determine the basic patterns of media ownership. We suggested that the relationship between media ownership and control is a complex one, not least because of the importance of state intervention and regulation. In this chapter, we examine the complex nature of this intervention and regulation, together with other important elements of control such as the processes of recruitment, selection and appointment. By concentrating on the broadcasting institutions, we can examine ways in which internal factors such as management structures, editorial policies, technical and financial operations, and the concept of professionalism, operate as important mechanisms of control.

The media in Britain are subject to a wide range of government legislation, some of which is directed specifically at it. This legislation determines the parameters within which media institutions are allowed to operate. For example, the 1954 Broadcasting Act established regional franchises for commercial broadcasting, what we have come to know as ITV. In a similar way, the 1984 Cable and Broadcasting Act legislates who is eligible to own and operate local TV franchises. Other legislation is more indirect, not being aimed specifically at the media, but establishing a legal framework within which both the press and broadcasting must operate. Good examples are the 1911 Official Secrets Act, the 1974 Prevention of Terrorism Act, and the 1981 Contempt of Court Act.

In addition to government legislation which has a direct controlling influence, media institutions in Britain are subject to a panoply of regulatory bodies. Many of these are supposed to ensure that the media are both accountable and representative, though all too often they fail to do this. For example, the Press Council, a self-regulatory body established by the newspaper owners, was criticised by the 1990 Calcutt Committee into Privacy and Related Matters for failing to curb the worst excesses of the tabloid press. Yet whilst the Report criticised falling standards in journalism, and replaced the Press Council with the Press Complaints Commission, it stopped short of recommending that an independent regulatory body be established, leaving effective control firmly in the hands of private ownership.

Broadcasting in Britain does have regulatory bodies which are largely independent of the broadcasting industry itself, but not from government. Social policy towards broadcasting in Britain since its establishment in the 1920s has been dominated by the notion of spectrum scarcity. The limited range of radio frequencies available for broadcasting was used as an argument for state regulation and control of the technological apparatus, as well as programme content. Broadcasting in Britain was created and continues to exist by courtesy of the state, though state control has been denied ideologically by regulatory structures which suggest that broadcasting is democratically accountable and independent. The most familiar of these structures centres around the appointment of representatives to serve as Governors of the BBC. Schlesinger (1987) argues that the Governors, who are appointed by the government, are 'an important point of articulation between the state and broadcasting'. The same comment could be said to apply to the appointed members of the Independent Broadcasting Authority (IBA) and its successor the Independent Television Commission (ITC).

The BBC has a governing body of 12, of whom one is Chairman, another Vice-Chairman, and three more are respectively National Governors for Scotland, Wales and Northern Ireland, all appointed for five years. Though constitutionally the appointments are made by the Queen-in-Council, in practice they are appointed by the Home Secretary. The BBC Annual Report claims that the Governors 'are drawn from a wide variety of background and experience, so as to represent the wider public interest'. The Governing Body is advised by an extensive network of General, Regional and Local Advisory bodies, members of which are selected by the Corporation itself.

The IBA has a maximum of 13 Members, including three who have specific responsibility for Scotland, Wales and Northern Ireland, all of whom are appointed by the Home Secretary. Here, too, the Members are advised by a General Advisory Council, as well as specialist committees on educational and religious broadcasting, charitable appeals and advertising.

Reference

P. Schlesinger (1987) *Putting 'Reality' Together*, 2nd edn, Constable, pp. 149–51.

☐ Relations between the Broadcasting Authorities and the Government

For some, this panoply of 'representative' bodies has been seen as broadcasting's guarantee of independence from Government and from potential self-interest by media professionals. In the following extract, written in 1981, Government powers over broadcasting are acknowledged, but are said to be circumscribed by the independence of the broadcasting authorities.

Reading 1

The constitutional relationship between the Government and the broadcasting authorities is concerned with programmes, finance, technical matters and the organization of the authorities. It provides the broadcasting authorities with independence in matters of programme content. This independence carries with it certain obligations as to programmes and programme standards. Each authority provides its respective radio and television services as public services for the dissemination of information, education and entertainment. They must ensure that their programmes display, as far as possible, a proper balance and a wide range of subject matter, accuracy in news coverage, impartiality in matters of controversy, and also that programmes should not offend against good taste or decency, or be likely to encourage crime and disorder, or be offensive to public feeling.

Since the earliest days of the BBC's service, successive governments have reaffirmed as fundamental the principle that governments treat their powers as major reserve powers only. The Government has the authority to prescribe the hours of broadcasting . . . to require the broadcasting of ministerial announcements and of any other matter in an emergency . . . ; to veto any particular broadcast or class of broadcast – this has always been regarded as a reserve power and only five directions of a general kind have ever been given and the Government has never used its powers to prevent a particular programme from being broadcast . . .

The governors of the BBC and the members of the IBA have the duty of providing their broadcasting services as public services in accordance with the terms of their respective governing instruments. For the performance of these duties the authorities are answerable to Parliament partly through ministerial responsibility to Parliament for the appointment and dismissal of members of the broadcasting authorities.

Source

Home Office (1981) *Broadcasting in the United Kingdom*, HMSO.

Questions

1. In what ways does the extract support the assumption that there is a consensus about the concept of 'good broadcasting'?
2. What does the extract imply about the extent of state control over British broadcasting?
3. Where does power and control reside in the constitutional relationship between the governors and members, and the Government?

☐ The Socio-economic Background of Appointees to Broadcasting Regulatory Bodies

This view about the independence of broadcasting from Government control has been called into question, even before recent direct interventions by the Government to alter or ban the transmission of programmes such as the *Secret Society* series (which examined, amongst other issues, secret defence satellites) and *Death On The Rock* (a documentary about the killing of three suspected IRA terrorists in Gibraltar). Heller (1978) points to problems involved in the selection and appointment process. Not only are those selected 'predominantly middle-class, middle-aged and until recently male', being part-time they are overly reliant on the professionals for information and advice, so that they are drawn into 'complicity in events and actions' which they have 'little opportunity to control or direct'. Some have argued that the appointment of Lord Chalfont, first as Deputy Chairman of the IBA and then as Chairman of the Radio Authority, represents an openly political appointment.

Reference

C. Heler (1978) *Broadcasting and Accountability*, British Film Institute.

Reading 2

Table 2.1   BBC board

			Occu-pation	Public School	Uni-versity	Ox-bridge
Chair						
Marmaduke Hussey		1986–	Bus	×	×	×
Stuart Young	(1981)	1983–86	Acc	–	–	–
George Howard	(1972)	1980–83	Land	×	×	×
Sir Michael Swan		1973–80	Acad	×	×	×
Vice-chair						
Lord Barnett		1986–	Acc/Pol	–	–	–
Sir William Rees-Mogg		1981–86	Journ	×	×	×
Hon Mark Bonham Carter		1975–81	PServ/Pol	×	×	×
Scotland						
Sir Graham Hills		1989–	Acad	–	×	–
William Watson Peat		1984–89	Farm	×	–	–
Sir Roger Young		1979–84	Teach	×	×	×
Prof. Alan Thompson		1976–79	Acad/Pol	–	×	–
Lady Avonside		1971–76	Lect	×	×	–
Wales						
John Parry		1986–	Vet	×	×	×
Alwyn Roberts		1979–86	Acad	–	×	–
Dr Glyn Tegai Hughes		1971–79	Acad	×	×	×
Northern Ireland						
Dr James Kincade		1985–	Teach	×	×	×
Lady Faulkner		1978–85	Journ	–	×	–
Members						
Keith Oates		1988	Bus/Acc	×	×	–
Bill Jordan		1988	TU	–	–	–
P. D. James		1988	CServ/Wr	–	–	–
Dr John Roberts		1988	Acad	×	×	×
Sir Curtis Keeble		1985	FO	–	×	–

Table 2.2   IBA board

			Occu-pation	Public School	Uni-versity	Ox-bridge
Chair						
George Russell	(1979)	1989–	Bus	–	×	–
Lord Thomson	(1980)	1981–88	PServ/Pol	–	–	–
Lady Plowden		1975–80	PServ	×	–	–
Deputy chair						
Lord Chalfont		1988–	Bus/Pol	–	–	–
Sir Donald Maitland		1986–89	FO	×	×	–
Sir John Riddell		1981–85	Bus/Pol	×	×	×
Christopher Bland		1972–80	Bus	×	×	×
Scotland						
John Purvis		1985–89	Bus	–	×	–
Rev Dr W. J. Morris		1979–84	Rel	–	×	–
Dr T. F. Carberry		1970–79	Acad	–	×	–
Wales						
Gwilym Peregrine		1982–89	LGov	–	×	–
Prof. Huw Morris-Jones		1976–82	Acad	×	×	–
Northern Ireland						
Prof. John Fulton		1987–	Acad	–	×	–
Jill McIvor		1980–87	Acad	×	–	–
Lord Blease		1974–79	TU	–	–	–
Members						
Pauline Mathias		1989–	Teach	–	×	–
Ranjit Sondhi		1987–	Acad	×	×	–
Lady Popplewell		1987–	PServ	×	×	×
Sir Anthony Joliffe		1987–88	Bus	–	–	–
Michael H. Caine		1984–89	Bus	×	×	×
Prof. Alexander Cullen		1982–89	Acad	–	–	–
Roy Grantham		1984–	TU	–	–	–

Table 2.3   Summary of Tables 2.1 and 2.2: 1974–89

	BBC %	IBA %
Men	79	70
Women	20	30
Private school	56	33
Oxbridge	49	21
Other university	23	36
Business/ accountancy	21	27
Education	31	33
Public sector	23	21
Trade unionist	10	12

Table 2.4 Broadcasting Standards Council

		Occu-pation	Public School	Uni-versity	Ox-bridge
Chair					
William Rees-Mogg	1988–	Journ	×	×	×
Deputy chair					
Jocelyn Barrow	1988–	Acad	–	×	–
Richard Baker	1988–	Journ	–	×	×
Dr Jean Curtis-Raleigh	1988–	Med	×	×	–
Alf Dubs	1988–	PServ	–	×	–
Dr R. Brinley Jones	1988–	Acad	–	×	×
Rev Charles Robertson	1988–	Rel	–	×	–
Rt Rev William Westwood	1988–	Rel	–	×	×

Table 2.5 Broadcasting Complaints Commission

		Occu-pation	Public School	Uni-versity	Ox-bridge
Chair					
Lady Anglesey	1987–	PServ	×	–	–
Tony Christopher	1989–	TU	–	–	–
David Holmes	1987–	Journ	×	–	–
Henry Mckenzie-Johnston	1986–	FO	×	–	–
Brigid Welles	1986–	Teach	–	×	×

Source: Tables 1–5, *The Guardian*, 15.1.90.

Questions

1. What general conclusions can be made about the socio-economic background of the governors and members?
2. Do these statistics support Heller's concern that there are problems involved in the selection and appointment of members serving on regulatory bodies? What might these problems be?
3. What arguments are there for having regulatory bodies like the Broadcasting Standards Council and the Broadcasting Complaints Commission?

□ An Alternative View of Broadcasting and the State

Lord Chalfont's business connections and his involvement with a number of avowedly right-wing pressure groups implied for many a shift beyond what has always been seen as the broadly establishment membership of the IBA and BBC, towards a closer identification with Government, its power and its policies. It has been argued that such appointments only bring into the open the real relationship between broadcasting and the state.

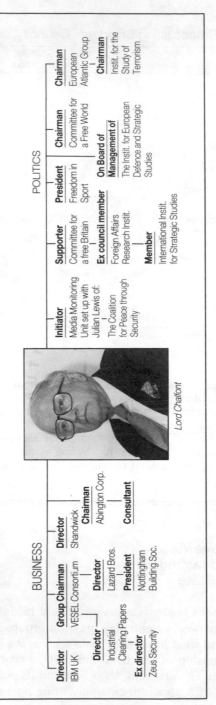

Figure 2.1 Lord Chalfont's business and political connections in 1989.
(Source: *The Guardian*, 4.2.89.)

Reading 3

The BBC's status as a public corporation has, in the past, obscured its identity as a creature of the state. If anyone doubts the reality of this legal dependence let them examine clause 13.4 of the BBC's licence, which was used by Douglas Hurd when enforcing the Northern Ireland ban. 'The Secretary of State may from time to time, by notice in writing, require the corporation to refrain at any specific time or at all times from sending any matter or matters of any class specified in such a notice.'

The BBC – this is a clear intention of its licence – has no recourse against this clause, because the secretary of state, who appoints the governors as custodians of a free institution at the service of the public, also has the power to dismiss them.

History shows that these powers create problems for the BBC and for governments. From the perspective of the state, the powers are so great that they are difficult to use, except in extreme circumstances. Phone calls to the governors, such as Leon Brittan's over *Real Lives*, are more usual. That is to the BBC's advantage, but it follows from the existence of such powers that the BBC must be careful not overly to provoke, or to do so only after carefully laying its ground.

The BBC's chosen line of defence has always been its mandate of impartiality. If the corporation can demonstrate a commitment to impartiality, that is some defence against the hand of the state. This was Reith's position in relation to the general strike, and it was used to defend the BBC during the Suez crisis. In the eighties, with a government which on a number of issues, explicitly identifies itself with the national interest, and with a fragmented national conscious-ness in which the concept no longer carries its old meaning, 'impartiality' has become progressively more difficult for the BBC.

What can you do when you can less and less serve your public while managing to please the state? Much of the opprobrium heaped first on Alistair Milne [Director-General until his resignation in 1987] and then on John Birt [Deputy Director-General since 1987] arises from this contradiction . . . Birt is now accused, through his definitions of good journalism, of having resolved it in favour of the Government ('We do cover the whole agenda, but it's an agenda set by the Government', says a critic). The argument is bitter because there is no real resolution.

Source

Nicholas Fraser (1989) 'Broadcasting's battle of conscience', *Broadcast*, 17 March.

Questions

1. (a) What evidence is there to support the view that the BBC is 'a creature of the state'?
   (b) What evidence could you use to refute this claim?
2. The relationship between the media and the state has been characterised as 'alternate moments of apparent autonomy and real subjection'. What is the role of state-appointed governors and members in this?
3. What arguments could be advanced for having elected governors and members, rather than them being selected and appointed by the Secretary of State for the Home Office?

☐ Conflict and Power within Media Organisations

The existence of appointed lay governors and members offers a theoretical independence from state control which is contradicted by actual events. This tension between independence and accountability at the constitutional level also operates within media organisations. For those working within the media industries, the conflict is articulated around appeals to professionalism and, particularly with those journalists working in news and current affairs, claims of impartiality. This tension and the language with which it is debated recognises genuine role conflicts, but usually stops short at acknowledging structural issues of power and control. Too often, media workers either do not see, or are unable to admit, that the organisational structures within which they work operate mechanisms of control which determine and influence their output. When bureaucratic organisational pressures do impinge upon their sense of 'professionalism', it is seen as an attack upon what they see as their creativity and autonomy.

Reading 4

The term 'professional' is commonly used in at least three different ways. First, there is the use of the term to denote the 'expert', in contrast to the 'amateur'. This is a usage found to be widespread in the BBC. Second, there is the Weberian view of the professional as the rational bureaucratic, efficient role embodying the concept of 'service' to the client or public. The third, Durkheimian use describes the way in which professionalism invest their work and organizations with moral values and norms.

It is often argued that a central dilemma for mass communicators concerns the extent to which the large-scale media organization tends to 'bureaucratize' the creative role of its members. Demands for stability, regularity and continuity may be said to drive media institutions towards the rationalization of staff roles – to create professionals in the sense described by Weber. However, it can also be argued that the negative effects of bureaucratization on individual roles can be countered by the development of professional pride and values – in the sense used by Durkheim – which may at times even run counter to the interests of the organization . . . It follows, therefore, that media 'professionalism', while perhaps arising from one basic source of conflict – that between organizational goal and creative occupational role – can actually be used to respond to that conflict in two quite different ways, which may themselves promote conflict.

Elliott (1977) suggests that claims to professionalism in the mass media represent, on the one hand, an *occupational adaptation* or response to the dilemmas of role conflict and, on the other, an *organizational strategy* to meet the demands of significant, consti- tuents in the environment of media institutions. Examining the contradictory demands of 'art' and 'commerce' in media institu- tions, Elliott points out that this simple dichotomy actually fuses a number of interrelated dilemmas for the communicator, notably the pursuit of ideas such as 'creativity' and 'autonomy' within organiza- tional milieus which may tend to foster more pragmatic responses to day-to-day events. The basic dilemmas are complex and may encompass such contradictory demands as those between high and low culture, professional standards and commercial judgement, self-regulation and bureaucratic control, self-motivation and finan- cial inducement, self-monitoring and serving an audience, using one's talents to some artistic, social or political purpose and having them used solely for the commercial ends of the organization. Given this complexity, the responses or adaptations made by communica- tors are equally complex. However, Elliott argues, the end result – the media output – will only vary if the response of the individual communicator is supported by the organizational system in which the communicator is working.

A focus on the twin dilemmas posed by the professional pursuit of 'creativity' and 'autonomy' within the organizational context raises a further dimension or set of tensions in relation to media production. This concerns the relative importance of structural and of operational factors in the development of media output. In a general sense, it should become clear that although structural considerations partly, at least, determine both the nature of mass media operations and the approaches adopted in their execution, in the main they impinge on the day-to-day implementation of individuals' roles. These are affected at least as much by immediate, operational considerations as by their structural location within the organization.

Source

Margaret Gallagher (1988) 'Negotiation of control in media organizations and occupations', in M. Gurevitch, T. Bennett, J. Curran and J. Woollacott (eds), *Culture, Society and the Media*, pp. 151–73.

Reference in Reading

P. Elliott (1977) 'Media organisations and occupations: an overview', in M. Gurevitch, J. Curran. J. Woollacott (eds), *Mass Communication and Society*, Edward Arnold.

Questions

1. Why might the development of the concept of 'professionalism' be important for media workers?
2. How meaningful is it to distinguish between the 'immediate operational considerations' influencing media workers and their 'structural location' within the organisation they work for?

☐ Other Features of Control within BBC News

Whilst the concept of professional autonomy is important and can lead to conflict with institutional values and strategies, as when, in 1990, a journalist resigned as a protest against *The Sun* printing faked pictures supposedly showing Channel Tunnel workers asleep at work, its importance can easily be overstated. Individual

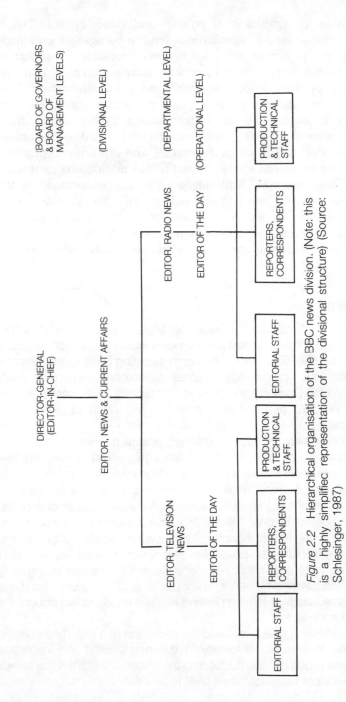

Figure 2.2 Hierarchical organisation of the BBC news division. (Note: this is a highly simplifiec representation of the divisional structure) (Source: Schlesinger, 1987)

opposition to organisational policies and values is rare. This is partly because media organisations tend to be rigidly hierarchical and so the power to hire and fire staff remains an important control mechanism, one that has been exercised on more than one occasion by both Robert Maxwell and Rupert Murdoch. Less dramatically, there are other pressures which encourage conformity. In his study on the production of news and current affairs programmes at the BBC, Schlesinger (1987, Reading 5) outlines ways in which organisational structure and institutional practices encourage consensus views of 'reality'. In addition to the formal 'command structure', Schlesinger notes the importance of the informal 'guidance' on editorial policy which filters down to staff by means of the minutes which record decisions made and opinions expressed at senior management meetings. Such 'guidance' is an important means of control, but there are others.

Reading 5

Apart from the diffusion of guidance, there are a number of factors which ensure the conformity of the news staff. First, it is important to realize that the BBC News has a high standing in the Corporation. It is prestigious, commanding larger resources, and ideologically central to the Corporation's 'mission'. Crucially, all its operatives are staff members of the BBC, with the exception of a very few free-lances.

Staff members are hard to dismiss, and all newsmen go through an extensive probationary period before they go on to the establishment. Each year an annual report is written on staff members which, if unsatisfactory, may result in the withholding of an increment . . . More significant is the attractiveness of a stable job in one of the bastions of the national culture. At a time of increasing casualization of labour in the media industries, with ever more staff going over to short-term contracts, BBC News is often viewed as a career structure in its own right. For many deskmen, the ultimate goal is one of the coveted assistant editor posts, and for reporters a move into a specialism or foreign posting is often an attractive option, if it can be achieved.

The diffusion of guidance and the attraction of a well-renumerated job tend to ensure conformity in the newsrooms. An important additional mode of control built into the editorial system is the power of sub-editors to assign news staff to stories.

Sub-editors have devolved control over discrete parts of the output, and the disposition of this control results from assignments made by the senior desk editors. As one put it: 'It's a complicated business taking into account preferences, ability, skills, knowledge, training'. By and large we can translate this into the crucial and opaque occupational criterion of 'experience'. The way assignments are given reflects the newsroom status structure: there is a pecking order for the allocation of stories. This order is based on an assessment by senior editors of a given newsman's reliability.

. . . In the allocation of work, the views of senior newsroom editors, especially editors of the day, are quite decisive. One sub told me how he had been labelled as 'unpromotable' by one editor of the day because their news judgement constantly diverged. The editor of the day had said that he could not feel confident that the sub would make the same decisions as he would in his place. The sub had set out to be more 'reliable' and had consequently been promoted.

When a newsman's performance is felt to be inadequate he is put on a periodic report, with reviews of progress every three or six months. This means that his reporting superior is required to keep an especially close eye on his work. Such sanctions are exceedingly rare . . . The more usual sanctions, apparently, are subtle ones. Thus some younger newsmen in Radio News whose ideas on news were too unorthodox were shown their superiors' displeasure. One sub was 'exiled to archives – rather like Siberia'. Another 'found I was doing the premium bonds and the cricket scores. That was a heavy hint.' Another ploy is to give people no work at all, or to put them on stories which are never used.

Source

P. Schlesinger (1987) *Putting 'Reality' Together*, 2nd edn, Routledge, pp. 149–51.

Questions

1. How persuasive are Schlesinger's arguments that informal, unarticulated elements of control are influential in constructing a consensual representation of news and current affairs? Give reasons for your answer.
2. To what extent do the reported comments of news journalists quoted in the extract suggest that they sense some hierarchy of news values? In what ways might such a sense of news values amongst media professionals be constructed?

□ The Socio-economic Characteristics of Media Professionals

Many would argue that staff recruitment tends to come from those social groups whose background and education is supportive of the establishment values embodied in the dominant media institutions. As Tunstall (1971) showed, the more prestigious journalism posts in the British media tend to be filled by graduates from Oxford, Cambridge and London. Although this is perhaps less the case in the 1990s, selection and recruitment throughout the media industry remains biased against women and heavily biased against ethnic minorities, so that they are severely under-represented in technical, production and executive posts.

Ethnographic studies such as those by Schlesinger (1987) and Elliott (1972) of media organisations and people working within them, do much to help us understand the importance of internal structures of control which encourage consensus and conformity, and lead us to question the relevance of notions of 'professional autonomy'. In much the same way, research into the socio-economic background of media professionals, and into patterns of recruitment, suggests that it is institutional, rather than individual, determinants which are of greater significance in media production.

It has been argued that recruitment patterns are changing. For example, recent studies of media professionals in the United States, such as those by Weaver and Wilhoit (1985), suggest that although more women are employed as journalists, the underlying conformity to established institutional values remains unchanged. We need to consider why it is, if recruitment patterns are changing, that this conformity continues.

References

P. Elliott (1972) *The Making of a Television Series – a Case Study in the Production of Culture*, Constable.
P. Schlesinger (1987) *Putting 'Reality' Together*, Methuen.
J. Tunstall (1971) *Journalists at Work*, Constable.
D. H. Weaver and G. Wilhoit (1985) *The American Journalist*, Indiana University Press.

Reading 6

Many studies of media organizations or occupations include, as a matter of course, an examination of the social background and outlook on society of the group of respondents under study. This is sometimes because of an assumption that the personal characteristics of those most responsible for media production will influence content. It is a hypothesis which accords well with the ideology of mythology of the media themselves and stands opposed to the notion of organizational or technological determinism. Inevitably there are as many descriptions of social background as there are studies and although most concern journalists, there is no single pattern to report.

However, a few general remarks are in order, taking as a starting point the findings of Weaver and Wilhoit [1985] concerning the social composition of American journalists in 1982–3 and using their definition of journalists as 'those who have editorial responsibility for the preparation or transmission of news stories or other information, including full-time reporters, correspondents, columnists, newsmen and editors'. It is clear that US journalists, however marginal their role in theory, are not marginal in income terms, but belong on average to the middle category, thus within the economically secure sector of society, without being rich. This mirrors . . . the data from Britain afforded by Tunstall.

Secondly, there are evidently big variations between the stars of journalism and the ordinary salariat, as in other branches of media business. Weaver and Wilhoit quote a study of 240 elite US news media personnel to the effect that demographically the elite is 'more secular, more white and more male than the country as a whole'. Johnson et al. (1976) are cited as concluding that 'in any society those in charge of mass communication tend to come from the same strata as those in control of the economic and political systems'. Interestingly, Weaver and Wilhoit themselves find that, since 1971, the composition of the corps of US journalists had changed remarkably in one respect – a much greater representation of women (from 20 to 34 per cent), although there were relatively fewer black and Hispanic journalists. There seems little doubt that the general class position of the average media worker – it is a middle-class occupation, but less professionalized or well paid than other established professions (law, medicine, accountancy, etc.) and with a small elite of well-paid stars . . .

The theoretical significance of these observations is less easy to interpret. One view ... is that the middle-class position of the journalistic profession is a guarantee of their ultimate loyalty to the system. Therefore they are free, in the American system, because they can be trusted to see and interpret the world in much the same way as the real holders of power, holding the same basic ideology and values. It is a persuasive view, more so than the alternative idea that they are not only an elite, but a left-leaning one with subversive motives, or alternatively a conservative elite (as some conspiracy theorists hold). More significant (and not inconsistent) may be the finding that media personnel owe most of their relevant attitudes and tendencies to socialization from the immediate work environment. This view, while not discounting the influence of social background and personal belief, returns us to the greater probability of organizational rather than individual subjective determination.

Source

D. McQuail (1987) *Mass Communication Theory: An Introduction*, 2nd edn, Sage, pp. 150–1.

References in Reading

J. W. L. Johnstone, E. J. Slawski and W. W. Bowman (1976) *The News People*, University of Illinois.

D. H. Weaver and G. Wilhoit (1985) *The American Journalist*, Indiana University Press.

Questions

1. What do you understand by the phrase 'the ideology or mythology of the media themselves'?
2. What generalisations, if any, does the reading make about the socio-economic background of media professionals?
3. It is suggested that even when recruitment patterns change, as with the greater number of women employed as media professionals, loyalty to the institution prevails. Why should this be?

☐ Media Freedom in the Dock

We have suggested that, quite apart from issues of ownership and control, media institutions are constrained in a number of ways.

Whatever talk there may be about 'independence', 'accountability' and 'professional autonomy', state legislation and control, together with organisational imperatives which operate upon media employees, ensure that media output is best characterised by conformity, consensus and an over-riding loyalty to dominant policies and values. Some commentators argue that the media's duty to provide information to the public is made increasingly difficult because of these various controls.

Reading 7

April was a wicked month for press and broadcasting freedom. There were a string of hostile police actions and court decisions which threaten the independence of the media from the state and the flow of information to the public.

Three weeks into the month and the Metropolitan Police had succeeded in gaining two court orders against no less than 29 news organizations forcing them to turn over published and unpublished film of the London Poll Tax disturbances of 31 March.

Sandwiched between these hearings the High Court imposed a £5000 fine on trainee journalist William Goodwin for contempt of court for refusing to reveal his source of confidential information about a company's financial affairs. The Law Lords had earlier rejected his appeal out of hand.

Mr Justice Hoffman made it clear that he included the newspaper owners Press Council and not just the National Union of Journalists (NUJ), in his strictures against a journalist's duty to protect his or her sources . . . Hoffman told Goodwin: 'All our freedom, including the freedom of the press, is based on law and public respect for the democratic procedures by which the law is made and changed'.

The hundreds of radical printers who went to prison rather than submit their publications to state censorship would have been greatly amused by this claim. Indeed, it is only the judiciary's particularly perverted reading of Section 10 of the 1981 Contempt of Court Act – which sought to prevent disclosure – which allowed the case against Goodwin to succeed by equating the commercial interests of a company with justice.

There is little doubt that Goodwin will win at the European Court of Human Rights using article 10 of the European Convention. Those caught in the police trawl through the photo files and film libraries of the Poll Tax disturbances are unlikely to be so fortunate.

Section 9 of the 1984 Police and Criminal Evidence Act was the first time in history that a specific legal procedure was laid down by which the police could seize film . . .

The independence of the media from the state – theoretical as this is at times – is a basic principle of a democratic state. The job of journalists, camera crews and photographers is to report events to supply the public with information, not collect evidence for the police. Once this independence is compromised press and broadcasting freedom is in double jeopardy.

Firstly, reporters and photographers become potential targets for an angry crowd and can be prevented from doing their job. Already on March 31 there were shouts of 'Maggie's boys' as one TV crew had its camera smashed. Secondly, the public's right to know is denied if editors, fearing either injury to reporters or police seizure of film, stop sending tems to potential trouble spots. And the free flow of information is the oxygen of democracy . . .

Further police powers over the media are on the way. When the Broadcasting Bill becomes law, only a magistrate's order will be needed for the police to use provisions of the Public Order and Obscene Publications Acts to seize copies of notes, scripts and tapes from radio and TV stations. With what independence there is left in broadcasting threatened by deregulation, the state is strengthened to ensure that the market is free, but thought is not.

Source

'Media Freedom in the Dock', *Free Press* (Journal of the Campaign for Press and Broadcasting Freedom), May/June 1990, p. 1.

Questions

1. In what ways is it suggested that the courts and the police are threatening freedom of information?
2. How does the article imply that British law is being interpreted and applied in ways which can be regarded as contrary to justice? Do you agree?
3. In what ways do court and police action prevent journalists, camera crews and photographers from reporting to the public?

□ Media
Reform

Concern about controls which inhibit the flow of information between the media and the public are matched by concern over issues such as media accountability, the public right of access to the media, and the public's right of reply. Earlier in this chapter we mentioned examples where direct Government intervention had prevented or modified the transmission of television programmes. These, together with what many people regard as the serious lowering of journalistic standards, especially in the British tabloid press, have led to calls for reform which would make the media more accountable to the public and allow greater public access, including a legal right of reply.

Reading 8

The overriding objectives of reform should be to conserve the existing strengths of the British media; increase its independence from both government and the expanding communications conglomerates; and extend the media's political and cultural diversity so that it is more representative of the different classes and subcultures that make up British Society.

A Ministry of Arts, Communications, and Entertainment (ACE) should be established to co-ordinate the development of a media, culture and leisure policy. It should be headed by a minister of Cabinet rank . . .

Steps should be taken to inject greater diversity into the British media by promoting the growth of a vigorous, independent sector which is controlled neither by powerful public agencies nor by the communication combines. This could be achieved by the following:

1. Require the BBC, ITV, and British satellite television channels to carry a specified quota of programmes made by independent UK production companies.
2. Franchise new local community radio stations.
3. Either restrict ownership of newspapers to EEC citizens and registered companies or limit joint ownership of national papers to only one national daily and Sunday paper. This should be accompanied by a statutory option period of three months in which the sale of divested publications is limited to employees

and independent consortia with no newspaper holdings.
4. Introduce grants for low advertising, low circulation national newspapers on the model pioneered in France.
5. Establish a Media Enterprise Board to aid the launch of new media companies and fund alternative ownership of divested media.

Of these five proposals, the last perhaps is the most important. The strategy of promoting the development of an independent media sector could amount to merely encouraging the growth of small businesses and, at worst, to encouraging the casualization of the media industry in a way that would threaten the security and living standards of people working in broadcasting. But it could also lead to a major enfranchisement of interests under-represented in the media *providing* a Media Enterprise Board is established to assist groups with limited capital to start media enterprises and buy up existing ones.

The introduction of an independent programme quota makes unnecessary a restructuring of the BBC and ITV since it encourages both networks to draw upon new inputs and experiences. However, a duty to 'present fairly and accurately important differences of interest and outlook within society' should be written into the terms of reference of both organizations. This would not supersede the requirement to maintain an overall balance in programme output but it would under-write an obligation on both networks to reflect a wider range of opinions and value systems than they do at present.

The media should also be distanced from the state. All members of broadcasting authorities should be elected through an electoral college instead of being appointed by the government. The Official Secrets Act should be reformed to cover only the betrayal of national security to a foreign power, and this should be accompanied by the introduction of a Freedom of Information Act.

Among the many other desirable legal reforms that have been proposed, the legal right of reply stands out as a measure which has extensive support across the political spectrum. It should be confined to corrections of factual misrepresentation, and cover both the press and broadcasting . . .

These proposals would not establish a fully democratic media system. But taken together, they would go some way towards creating media with power *and* responsibility – to the public rather than to proprietors and governments.

Source

J. Curran and J. Seaton (1988) *Power Without Responsibility: The Press and Broadcasting in Britain*, 3rd edn, Routledge, pp. 320–2.

Questions

1. According to the writers, why is there a need for media reform?
2. What are the main legal and structural changes proposed in this programme for reform?
3. Some of the changes recommended here, such as the introduction of a quota for independently produced programmes to be shown on both BBC and ITV, have already happened, but the objectives outlined by the writers have not been realised. Why might this be?

General Questions

1. It has been said that broadcasting is too important to be left to the broadcasters. What bodies exist which act as public watchdogs, and how effective are they?
2. Examine the view that increased government legislation has seriously impaired the ability of the British media to report issues, events and ideas adequately.
3. Examine the view that professionalism serves the interests of professionals themselves rather than their clients. (*AEB 1986*)
4. Considering the content of the British press, how seriously should we take the concept of professionalism?
5. Examine sociological explanations of the processes involved in the selection and presentation of the news. (*AEB 1990*)
6. Critically examine evidence for the view that reporting of news is 'inevitably biased and selective'. Illustrate your answers with examples. (*AEB 1989*)
7. Is there a strong case for media reform?

Further Reading

M. Alvarado and J. Stewart (1985) *Made For Television-Euston Films Ltd*, BFI/Methuen.

T. Burns (1970) 'Public Service and Private World', in *Media Sociology*, J. Tunstall (ed.), Constable.

T. Burns (1972) 'Commitment and Career in the BBC', in *Sociology of Mass Communications*, D. McQuail (ed.), Penguin.

J. Curran (1977) 'Capitalism and control of the press 1800–1975', in *Mass Communication and Society*, J. Curran, M. Gurevitch and J. Woollacott (eds), Edward Arnold.

P. Elliott (1977) 'Media organizations and occupations: an overview', in

Mass Communication and Society, J. Curran, M. Gurevitch and J. Woollacott (eds), Edward Arnold.

C. Heller (1978) *Broadcasting and Accountability*, British Film Institute.

K. Kumar (1977) 'Holding the middle ground', in *Mass Communication and Society*, J. Curran, M. Gurevitch and J. Woollacott (eds), Edward Arnold.

M. Morrison and H. Tumber (1988) *Journalists at War*, Sage.

G. Murdock (1988) 'Large corporations and the control of the communications industries', in *Culture, Society and the Media*, M. Gurevitch, T. Bennet, J. Curran and J. Woollacott (eds), Routledge.

J. Tunstall (1971) *Journalists at Work*, Constable.

3 Reality, representation and ideology

Enzenberger argues (1974) that every use of the media presupposes manipulation. There is no such thing as unmanipulated writing, filming or broadcasting. The question is not whether the media are manipulated, but who manipulates them, in whose interests, for what purposes and does this manipulation actually have any effects? So we begin by asking if the media can ever just portray reality without being involved in constructing it in a particular way, and thus being involved in ideological construction.

The earliest theories on the media tended to lay stress on the power of the media to turn people into a zombified mass who would respond to whatever the media suggested and believe whatever they were told. The theories of the German Frankfurt school assumed that there was one dominant ideology, which could be transmitted effectively to the masses. Basically, the critical theorists of this tradition believed that everyone was being 'conned', a position similar to that outlined in Chapter 1 which assumed that people suffer from false consciousness. This particular idea is still prevalent: Reggie Hudlin, a radical black film director notes:

> It's terrifying. You know what the worst drug is in America now? It's not narcotics, it's television – the bland speaking to the bland. (*The Guardian*, 30.8.90, p. 25)

This position has been developed into a more sophisticated analysis beginning with the work of Althusser (1977). He argued that the media was just one of the state's ideological apparatuses, like the church and schools, which were used to control people by giving them particular ideas and frameworks through which they could identify themselves. We gain a sense of who and what we are from the images that are available to us. We may, in fact, want to be like the total image that is on offer; hence the importance of 'lifestyle' marketing in which every aspect of a person's life can be defined through the products they use. Or we may recognise aspects of ourselves in images and subsequently believe ourselves to be part of the image. In both cases we have been called into a recognition that contributes to how we define ourselves. This recognition must always be limited and framed by what is available. Althusser calls this process interpellation.

This analysis has been developed further by use of Gramsci's (1971) notion of hegemony. Hegemony is the process by which people give their consent to the social system. It is used to explain how people agree to being part of a system which is clearly not in their interests. Gramsci argued that hegemony is so entrenched in society that it comes to define what most people consider to be common sense. So rather than having ideology imposed on them, hegemony suggests a more active role for individuals in which they believe they have constructed their ideas (the ideology) themselves. The theory of hegemony also suggests that consent has to be continually 'won'. The media plays an important part in this process, for they are able to reach the majority of the population with specific ideas. They also exclude other ways of seeing things.

It could be argued that people give their consent, because they do not know of any other way of behaving. For people to challenge the hegemony they would have to have some idea of effective protest and alternative ways of living. Even when alternatives are present, Williams (1973, Reading 3) argues that the media have the power to incorporate any challenges. He would argue that because punk became a viable commercial proposition, it was therefore incorporated into the system. This, however, does not take into account the wider repercussions of alternative movements. Even if punk bands have been incorporated into the commercial mainstream, this does not guarantee that their audience has also. Their effect may be to actually transform existing social relationships (as Burchill and Parsons show in Reading 5).

Grossberg (1988) claims that there will always be 'wars of position' between the rulers and the ruled (who, he maintains, are not an undifferentiated mass, but also divided). He argues that the rulers have to negotiate, either socially or commercially, with those who present a potential threat and are in opposition to the present system, but that this does not mean that they have been incorporated. They may remain in opposition. This is a more optimistic view, which allows space for change.

Bourdieu (1971) adds another dimension to this. He argues that our responses to the media, and other ideological apparatuses are premised upon our prior social experience. He identifies this as a two-way process in which the media and other social experiences are continually being measured against each other. This suggests that even if the media only provide one particular point of view, it will be weighed against our knowledge and experience to see if it is viable, or to see if we can actually benefit, and increase our cultural standing from taking it on board. The taking up of oppositional positions, such as rebellious music and politics, is often a means by which credibility can be gained and social reputation enhanced. This theory does enable us to stop thinking of the media as a separate unity set against people's social experiences. They are deeply entwined and part of the same process.

Williamson (1978, Reading 1) argues that advertisements subject us to ideological control. By selling us commodities advertisements also sell us ideas about ourselves. Drawing on Althusserian theories of ideology, she argues that advertisements have the power to influence how we make sense of the world. In this way they effectively control us whilst encouraging us to buy.

References

L. Althusser (1977) *For Marx*, New Left Books.

P. Bourdieu (1971) *Outline of a Theory of Practice*, Cambridge University Press.

H. Enzenberger (1974) *The Consciousness Industry*, Seabury Press.

A. Gramsci (1971) *Selections from the Prison Notebooks of Antonio Gramsci*, Q. Hoare and G. Nowell-Smith (trans and eds) Lawrence and Wishart.

L. Grossberg (1988) *It's a Sin: Essays on Postmodernism, Politics, Culture*, Power Publications.

☐ Advertisements: Selling Us Ourselves?

Reading 1

Advertisements are one of the most important cultural factors moulding and reflecting our life today. They are ubiquitous, an inevitable part of everyone's lives: even if you do not read a newspaper or watch television, the images posted over our urban surroundings are inescapable. Pervading all the media, but limited to none, advertising forms a vast superstructure with an apparently autonomous existence and an immense influence.

It is this ubiquitous quality and its tenacity as a recognisable 'form', despite the fact that it functions within different technical media and despite different 'content' (that is, different messages about different products), that indicates the significance of advertising. Obviously it has a function, which is to sell things to us. But it has another function, which I believe in many ways replaces that traditionally fulfilled by art or religion. It creates structures of meaning. The definition 'to sell things to us' – involves a meaning process. Advertisements must take into account not only the inherent qualities and attributes of the products they are trying to sell, but also the way in which they can make those properties *mean something to us*.

In other words, advertisements have to translate statements from the world of things, for example, that a car will do so many miles per gallon, into a form that means something in terms of people. Suppose that the car did a high mpg: this could be translated in terms of thriftiness, the user being a 'clever' saver, in other words *being a certain kind of person*. Of if the mpg was low, the ad could appeal to the 'above money pettiness', daredevil kind of person who is too 'trendy' to be economising. Both the statements could be made on the purely factual level of a 'use-value' by the simple figures of 50 mpg and 20 mpg. The advertisement translates these 'thing' statements to us as human statements; they are given a humanly symbolic 'exchange-value'.

Advertisements rather provide a structure which is capable of transforming the language of objects to that of people and vice-versa. Advertising sets up connections between certain types of consumers and certain products; and having made these links and created symbols of exchange it can use them as 'given' and so can we. So the connection of people and objects, the two do become interchangeable ... Advertisements are selling us something else beside consumer goods; in providing us with a structure in which we, and those goods, are interchangeable, they are selling us ourselves ... We are not participants in an ideology until we are active within its very creation; paradoxically ideology means that we are participants. In the process of the ad's 'saying' this and your 'understanding' it, the active subject has been created by assumption. When you understand the advert you have been hailed, what Althusser defines as interpellation, which is simply the 'Hey, you!' process of ideological apparatuses calling individual subjects. The point about 'Hey, you!' is that whenever you are called, you must already be.

Source

J. Williamson (1978) *Decoding Advertisements: Ideology and Meaning in Advertising*, Marion Boyars, pp. 11–13.

Questions

1. Williamson suggests that adverts create structures of meaning. How do they do this? What examples can you give?
2. Williamson assumes that just because adverts address us we automatically answer. Must all adverts be ideological, and hence involve social control of some kind?
3. Is it possible to be addressed in different ways by different adverts? What would this suggest about ideological control?

☐ Ideological Subversion?

Myers, in the next reading, argues against Williamson's idea (Reading 1) that people take on ideological messages intact. She believes that buying commodities is a way of dealing with dissatisfaction. This does not mean that people have been taken in by the intended meanings of the advert. Rather, she argues, people use commodities to their own advantage, to create their own style.

Reading 2

Myers (1986) examines the assumptions behind how ideology is used in the Williamson's explanation. Under the academic wing of Althusser, ideology became an all-embracing value system from which there was no escape. Ideology, according to Althusser, subsumed all of democracy's information systems: the media, education, art and the welfare state were all supporting and, worse still initiating ideologies which deadened the soul, brainwashed the mind, and made revolution a decade further away.

The media, and especially that spinner of affluent fantasies – advertising – had become the enemy . . . Judith Williamson said of the affluent worker: Thus instead of being identified by what they produce, people are made to identify themselves with what they consume . . . What an ad means depends on how it operates, how signs and its ideological effect are organised internally (within a text) and externally (in relation to production, circulation, consumption and in relation to technological, economic and social relations). The advert is treated as concentrated ideology, reinforcing certain values at the expense of others. Individualism, affluence and beauty take priority over, for example, basic information on how a machine works. Semiology, (the method that Williamson uses) then, is a method for identifying the signifiers (usually objects, words or scenes) in an advert which sets off chains of ideas in the mind of the reader . . . by arguing that the reader is far from an impartial observer. Rather, by virtue of looking at an advert, they enter into a contract with it. By completing the meaning of associated scattered elements (rather like a crossword puzzle) they've entered into the world of the advertisement . . . Rather, it is the subtle substitution of an object for a dissatisfaction. Consumption becomes a displacement and a solution. The image is pleasurable in its own right, not an incentive to action, but rather an alternative to it . . . Punks didn't 'need' safety pins but they were useful, partly because they held together two sections of clothing; and partly because they had an easily identifiable – and challengeable – social meaning. The 'enfant terrible' of this culture cannibalism is *The Face* magazine, essentially a catalogue of alternative lifestyle, a vision of cultural consumption (music, fashion, dis-information) severed from a clear sense of the economy. *The Face* therefore represents the acceptable face of disaffection, of a youth elite bordering affluent poverty who have no respect for the material values of bourgeois society. *Face* readers consume, but in terms of mainstream media they see themselves as a counter-culture, running against the grain of acceptability.

Source

K. Myers (1986) *Understains . . . the Sense and Seduction of Advertising*, Comedia, pp. 98, 100, 102, 139–40, 143, 151.

Questions

1. Is it possible to sell goods (an imperative of capitalism) without selling ideas? Give reasons for your answer.
2. Does buying commodities to displace dissatisfaction necessarily enable the consumers to challenge or resist ideological control?
3. Are *Face* readers or punks outside of ideological control because they

are subverting the meanings of the symbols by not using them for their advertised/intended purpose?

☐ Hegemony and Incorporation

Williams (1973), however, would argue that buying to displace dissatisfaction and subverting symbols are part of the process of hegemonic control. So people 'feel' as if they are being subversive, but in this process become incorporated into that which they thought they were challenging. From this analysis Punk can be seen as a fashion that was sold to those who wanted to believe they were rebellious and different.

Reading 3

Hegemony supposes the existence of something which is truly total, which is not merely secondary or superstructural, like the weak sense of ideology but which is lived at such a depth, which saturates the society to such an extent, and which, as Gramsci put it, even constitutes the limit of common sense for most people . . . Hegemony is not singular; indeed its own internal structures are highly complex, and have continually to be renewed, recreated and defended. By the same token, they can be continually challenged and in certain respects modified. That is why instead of speaking simply of 'the hegemony', 'a hegemony', I would propose a model which allows for this kind of variation and contradiction, its sets of alternatives and its processes of change . . . It is a whole body of practices and expectations; our assignments of energy, our ordinary understandings . . . It is a set of meanings and values which, as they are experienced as practices, appear as reciprocally confirming. It thus constitutes a sense of reality . . . We can only understand an effective and dominant culture if we understand the real social process on which it depends: I mean the process of incorporation. The modes of incorporation are of great social significance . . . Thus we have to recognise the alternative meanings and values, the alternative opinions and attitudes, even some alternative senses of the world which can be accommodated and tolerated within a particularly effective and dominant culture . . . I have next to introduce a distinction between *residual* and *emergent* forms, both of alternative and oppositional culture. By 'residual' I mean that some experiences, meanings and values which cannot be verified or cannot be expressed in the terms of the dominant culture, are nevertheless lived and practised on the basis of the residue – cultural as well as social – of some previous social formation . . . By 'emergent' I mean, first, that new meanings and values, new practices, new significances and experiences, are continually being created. But there is then a much earlier attempt to incorporate them, just because they are part – and yet not part – of effective contemporary practice. We have then to see, first, as it were, a temporal relation between a dominant culture, and on the one hand a residual and on the other hand an emergent culture . . . There is a simple theoretical distinction between alternative and oppositional, that is to say, between someone who simply finds a different way to live and wishes to be left alone with it, and someone who finds a different way to live and wants to change the society in its light.

Source

R. Williams (1973) 'Base and superstructure in Marxist cultural theory', in *New Left Review*, 82, December, pp. 3–16.

Questions

1. What is the difference between theories of hegemony which assume a dominant culture and dominant ideology theories?
2. Why does consent have to be continually won?
3. How does the hegemonic model account for change? How would this compare to ideological theories (see Williamson, Reading 1)?

□ The Nation

One of the most effective means for winning consent to a specific social order is to exclude, or delegitimate any alternative voices or ways of being. This can be achieved either through exclusion, through discreditation or through the construction of boundaries to a debate. The concept of 'the nation' is a powerful example of how certain forms of address make opposition and criticism difficult.

Reading 4

Perhaps the largest unity with which viewers are encouraged to identify themselves on television is the nation. Once again, the way we are implicated in the image of the nation is twofold. We see representations of it, from ceremonial occasions to a constantly reiterated repertoire of signifiers for England (which usually means Britain, and vice versa). Such signifiers range from the national flag to landscapes, people, music and objects that are regarded and treated as 'representing' England/Britain. There are equivalents for the other home nations – Wales, Scotland and Ireland – though their development is both less common and more equivocal and perhaps even more strongly stereotyped. Collecting emblems of each of the four nations, or of Britain as a whole, would show what makes up the image being represented.

The second way in which we are implicated in the nation is by the *relational* devices. When a newsreader speaks of 'we', there is a deliberate confusion between 'we' the participants in the event I'm describing, and 'we' (including *you*) the nation. In the context of American TV news, Robert Stam discusses the implications of this:

> Television news promotes what might be called . . . the regime of the 'fictive We' . . . Television, if not received critically, fosters a kind of confusion of pronouns: between 'I' the spectator and 'He' or 'She' the newscaster, as engaged in a mutually flattering dialogue. This fictive We can then speak warmingly about 'Ourselves' and coldly about whoever is posited as 'Them'. This misrecognition of mirror-like images has profound political consequences. Oil corporation commercials tell us: 'We Americans have a lot of oil.' The 'We' is clearly fictive; most of us own no oil; we buy it at exorbitant prices in the wake of a stage-managed energy crisis. Shortly after the ill-fated 'rescue attempt' in Iran (to free the American hostages in 1982), Chuck Scarborough of New York's *Channel 4 News* began his newscast, 'Well, we did our best, but we didn't make it.' The 'We' in this case presumably included the newscaster, the president (Carter) and a few aides. It certainly did not include the majority of Americans, even if their 'support' could be artfully stimulated after the fact. Television news, then, claims to speak for us, and often does, but just as often it deprives us of the right to speak by deluding us into thinking that its discourse is our own. Often it gives us the illusion of social harmony, the ersatz communication of a

global village which is overwhelmingly white, male and corporate.

Source

J. Hartley, H. Goulden and T. O'Sullivan (1985) *Making Sense of the Media*. Block Three. Unit Two: Audiences and Identities, Comedia, pp. 21–2.

Questions

1. Identify the two different techniques that implicate us in identifying ourselves as part of the British nation.
2. How does TV news claim to speak for us? What are the consequences of this?
3. In whose interests are the concepts 'we' and 'the nation' constructed? Give reasons for your answer.

☐ Sex, Violence and Subversion

Williams (Reading 3) would argue that punk music operated on a similar bias. It was the means by which those with commercial power were able to use young people's frustration and sell it back to them in a new package, incorporating them into the capitalist system in the process, and deflating all attempts at rebellion. Burchill and Parsons (1987) disagree. Although punk was commercialised and sold, they show how it challenged traditional forms of dressing and behaviour, paving the way for different attitudes to performance, music and sex.

Reading 5

McLaren and Westwood had gleaned sufficient experience of the working world which existed outside of their sheltered theories to realise that the generation gap would never get their names on the front of the Sunday papers, let alone shake the foundations of civilisation. After a radical reconsideration of shock tactics, they hit upon *Sex* (the shop) as the ultimate bastion of public inhibition and outrage. Their creations flaunted the subject matter of surreptitious plain brown wrapper titillation not to cater for the secret desires of guilt ridden respectable perverts but to shock indifferent and dismissive elders into white-knuckled, cardiac-arrest indignance. *Sex* output included T-shirts bearing extracts of hard-core porn prose and numerous pictorial depravities.

None of these clothes were either designed or worn to make the customer look alluring; on the contrary, the flagrant fashion in which the clothes used sex as an offensive weapon required a certain asexuality on the part of the wearer. They used sex not to entice but to horrify, the perfect expression of which was found in Jordan 'Don't call me Pamela' Hook, the *Sex* salesgirl who wore cutaway-buttock plastic leotards with black suspender belt and thigh boots while striving to make her hair, face and body as puke-promotingly repulsive as possible . . .

Rock had always flirted with violence as mere metaphor; (Johnny) Rotten destroyed the pose, and replaced it with the reality – constantly haranguing the audience with streams of abuse, spitting and snarling lyrics as though they tasted of his own piles, dancing like a rotten corpse still shaking from snarling its yarbles on the lid of a closing coffin, glassy eyes burning, pallid flesh decorated with self inflicted fag burns, amphetamine parched lips turned back in savage contempt as he went for the jugular – sometimes literally.

The Pistols had crystallised widespread repression, giving it form, style and dirootion. Single-handed, they had instigated a movement . . . By that summer, Punk Rock had evolved to the stage where it would be officially recognised by the rock establishment as a genuine new order.

Source

J. Burchill and T. Parsons (1987) *The Boy Looked at Johnny: the Obituary of Rock and Roll*, Pluto Press, pp. 29–35.

Questions

1. How did punk challenge the attitudes and styles previously associated with sexual attraction?
2. What reasons do Burchill and Parsons give to suggest that punk created a new musical order?
3. What evidence do Burchill and Parsons provide to suggest that the process of incorporation may not be achieved just because a band is commercially successful?

☐ Habitus and Distinction

All the previous readings have examined how the media user is addressed and why. They show how the user is framed by certain forms of address. This final extract from Garnham and Williams (1990) draws upon Bourdieu's work (1971, p. 45) to examine why it is that people are likely to respond to ideology in particular ways. It needs reading very carefully.

Reading 6

Bourdieu argues that any explanation of human action takes place in time. Audiences are already located. He argues that individuals are always placed in situations in which they will be uncertain of the outcomes (because their strategies are opposed by the strategies of others) thereby they have to draw upon certain strategies to operate in a particular situation. Bourdieu argues that these strategies are objectively coordinated by mechanisms unknown to the individual. He calls this regulating mechanisms the habitus. This he describes as: 'the strategy-generating principle enabling agents [individuals] to cope with unforseen and ever-changing situations . . . a system of lasting, transposable dispositions which, integrating past experiences, functions at every moment as a matrix of perceptions, apperceptions and actions and makes possible the achievement of infinitely diversified tasks, thanks to the analogical transfer of schemes permitting the solution of similarly shaped problems.

Garnham and Williams (1990) argue that the habitus is not just a random series of dispositions but operates according to a relatively coherent logic, what Bourdieu calls the logic of practice. This logic is shaped primarily in early childhood within the family by the internalization of a given set of determinate objective conditions both directly material and material as mediated through the habitus and thus the practices of surrounding adults. While later experience will alter the structure of the habitus's logic of practice, these alterations from school or work will be appropriated according to the logic of the habitus . . . The habitus is a unified phenomenon. Thus the habitus is a family, group and especially class phenomenon, a logic derived from a common set of individuals in common response to those conditions. The logic of practice does not reflect just individual reactions to the social environment but on the contrary are realistic assessments, in terms of the habitus, of the objective probabilities offered by a given state of the social field to an actor in a given class position. So when Bourdieu turns to the specific field of cultural consumption or rather appropriation, the regularities of his survey data reveal taste patterns across a wide range of goods as markers of the habitus of classes and class fractions . . . Thus the function of symbolic systems is to represent in a misrecognized form the structure of class relations. The symbolic system at once represents class relations and in the same movement disguises that representation because their logic is that of 'distinction' . . . What is also at stake is the legitimizing and deligitimizing of power. There is a tendency for the symbolic field to legitimize a given state of class relations by means of the mechanism of misrecognition by which symbolic systems represent in a 'euphemized', 'disinterested' form its balance of forces and hierarchical structure . . . Human agents enter the social formation with historically given endowments, either in an incorporated state within the habitus as dispositions and competencies, or in an objectified state as material goods. It is these endowments that Bourdieu refers to as capital, divided into economic and cultural capital. Each agent enters the struggle with the aim of reproducing the capital of his or her group and if possible augmenting it. To this end she or he pursues strategies of investment which involve choosing the subfields and the modes of intervention in those subfields likely to yield the highest profit on a given investment, one of the objects of struggle being the relative returns to an investment in a given field *vis-à-vis* investments in other fields.

Source

N. Garnham and R. Williams (1990) 'Pierre Bourdieu and the sociology of culture: an introduction', in N. Garnham (ed.), *Capitalism and Communication: Global Culture and the Economics of Information*, Sage, pp. 70–89.

Questions

1. What is 'habitus'?
2. How can your use of the media be used to increase cultural capital?
3. How is the habitus of the individual likely to influence their responses to the media?

General Questions

1. Is it inevitable that the media will manipulate? Use examples from the readings to support your argument.
2. The mass media may not tell us what to think, but they do tell us what to think about. Explain and discuss. (*AEB 1986*)
3. The mass media do not simply provide information and reflect the social world – rather they structure it for us, not simply increasing our knowledge of the world but helping us to 'make sense of it'. Discuss with reference to *one* area of social life. (*AEB 1984*)
4. How is an individual's social location likely to influence their responses to media output?

Further Reading

M. Barker (1989) *Comics: Ideology, Power and the Critics*, Manchester University Press.

J. Ellis (1982) *Visible Fiction: Cinema, Television, Video*, Routledge.

D. McQuail (1987) *Mass Communications Theory: An Introduction*, Sage, 2nd edn.

A. McRobbie (1991) *Feminism and Youth Culture: From Jackie to Just Seventeen*, Macmillan.

L. Masterman (1984) *Television Mythologies: Stars, Shows and Signs*, Comedia.

K. Myers (1986) *Understains. The Sense and Seduction of Advertising*, Comedia.

J. Williamson (1978) *Decoding Advertisements. Ideology and Meaning in Advertising,* Marion Boyars.

4 Representation: gender, race, class and age

The media are able to define what is 'natural' and 'normal' by associating certain social groups with particular behaviour. For instance when Metropolitan police figures were released on violent crime, many newspaper reports chose to focus on headlines such as ONE IN THREE MUGGERS IN BRITAIN ARE BLACK; they failed to mention that this must mean that two out of every three muggers were white. Defining what is 'normal' implicitly involves defining what is 'abnormal'. Hence women are often defined as neurotic, Blacks as volatile, Arabs as erratic and brutal. These definitions, perpetrated over a period of time and rarely challenged in the media, become so ubiquitous that we come to see them as part of our everyday common sense.

By defining the boundaries of the 'normal' and 'natural' gender and race appear to be given by nature, thus sexism and racism appear as the most profoundly naturalised of existing ideologies (Parmar, 1985). Hartmann and Husband (1974) in a classical study found that the popular response to black people was shaped significantly by the meanings provided by the mass media. They argue that the media created a social agenda around particular issues and framed the way they could be spoken about. The media provide the only source of information about black people for white people who have had little or no contact with them.

Unless our everyday experience of these groups enables us to contradict and challenge the labels that are given, the media may provide us with the only knowledge we have. Thus, the media is able to establish and legitimate particular ways of speaking about groups and delegitimate others. It can be a very powerful influence on how we categorise other people and respond to them. Consequently, the media operates as a form of social regulation which limits the ways in which we can understand groups and events. If the explanations and frameworks that are provided by the media are confirmed in other sites, such as the family and education, they may exert a more powerful influence.

Analysis of the content of the media enables us to examine the frequency of representation of these particular groups. It does not, however, enable us to analyse the type of representation. The word representation is used because it contains within it the idea that people are being re-presented to others and themselves. Sihera (1990) conducted a content analysis of 30 weeks of peak time television. Her report shows that on average 92 per cent of the BBC's output did not feature any black people, while for ITV with Channel 4, it was 94 per cent. Of the BBC's 8 per cent which portrayed black people, only 3.5 per cent was positive compared with ITV's 4.5 per cent. She notes that examined closely, while they purport to be portraying positive images of black viewers, they actually end up presenting black people as problems. It is therefore also important to bear in mind what is actually being excluded from the image that is being constructed.

For a number of years the Women's Media Action Group's monitoring of the media has found a catalogue of derogatory images, which primarily define women through their appearance. This should not be surprising when a report by the Institute of Practitioners in Advertising (1990) found that the whole industry was imbued with a sexist male ethos. A study for the Broadcasting Standards Council (1990) argues that 'the portrayal of women in television commercials shows the very unacceptable face of sexism'. Stereotyping is robust, 'lending strong support to the concern that women exist in what is essentially a man's world'. The study found that while most people were categorised as ordinary, the slim, model or 'ideal' category was applied to only one in ten men, compared with more than one in three women. The study suggests that women occupy a decorative role far more frequently than is the case with men. Men were also portrayed as 'humorous' while women were 'glamorous'.

The type of portrayal of particular groups enables certain attitudes to be legitimised. The above examples show how sexism is represented as 'normal'. Representations of masculinity often endorse the use of violence against women. Likewise racist representations, which construct black people as a problem and a threat, enable repressive state measures to be used against them in such a way as to make these responses appear to be legitimate. Reading 5 on racism, and the accompanying extract from *The Sun*, illustrate how the media is able to frame debates and close off criticisms by delegitimating any attempts that are made to challenge the status quo.

The reading on the 'New Man' (Reading 4) demonstrates how changes in masculinity were incorporated into an already existing definition of masculinity, which enabled the boundaries of masculinity to be stretched without losing any of the power that would traditionally be associated with it. We now have different representations and discourses of masculinity, which range from the traditional tough model to the vain and appearance-obsessed, narcissistic one.

The establishment of frameworks through media representations thus provides us with ways of understanding ourselves as well as other people: both Jane Root (Reading 1) and Richard Dyer (Reading 3) point out how representations of femininity and masculinity can be so restricting as to create long-term anxieties.

References

T. Hartman and C. Husband (1974) *Racism and the Media*, Davis-Poynter.

P. Parmar (1985) 'Hateful contraries: media images of Asian women', *Ten 8*, Vol. 16, pp. 71–8.

☐ Being Judged by Appearances

The following reading explores how advertising images encourage and feed off the sensation of what has been called 'to-be-looked-at-ness'. This, Root (1984, below) argues, is the fundamental means by which sexism is reinforced in the media, because women are made to feel constantly aware of being assessed in terms of how they look, their appearance, rather than what they actually do.

Reading 1

An analysis of women's representations began by exploring John Berger's (1972) work. He asserts:

> *men act* and *women appear*. Men look at women. Women watch themselves being looked at. This determines not only most relations between men and women but also the relation of women to themselves. The surveyor of woman in herself is

male: the surveyed female. Thus she turns herself into an
object – and most particularly an object of vision: a sight . . .

because how she appears to others, and ultimately how she
appears to men, is of crucial importance for what is normally
thought of as the success of her life . . . Images show females as
sexualised bodies, whose status in the world, and position in the
advertisement, is dependent on how they look rather than what they
do. Achievement is primarily visual achievement, and perfection is
the attainment of physical beauty. But, at the same time, advertisements aimed at women frequently offer the chance to *create* such
effect by the purchase of a particular product. Through the advertisement the woman is encouraged to enjoy a fantasy of power. But
unlike advertisements directed at men, this is not the power over
people and things, but the power of becoming a perfect *sight*, the
ultimate to-be-looked-at-women. Kathy Myers (1986) expands this
idea by writing that

> One of the pleasures which the advertising industry offers
> women is the promise of a kind of power and self-
> determination. Images of women marketed to women rarely
> present female sexuality purely in terms of vulnerability, acces-
> sibility or availability. But the power which the advertising of
> beauty and personal products offers women is always of a
> limited kind, located in terms of sexual display, appearance
> and attractiveness.

Rosalind Coward (1984) suggests that advertising encourages
women to see their bodies as a kind of *project, a task which can
always be improved or embellished*. This is particularly clear in the
advertisements common in women's magazines which only show a
small part of the body . . . Here the message is that each small
section of the body needs care and attention so that eventually it
can become as perfect as the carefully lit and heavily made-up arm,
lip, eyelid, thigh or foot in the photograph . . . The whole outer
surface of the body is transformed into an exquisite, passive *thing*.

These advertising images remain long after the actual product
and the specific claims made for it have been forgotten. For women,
the barrage of beautiful and sexualised bodies and parts of bodies
almost inevitably produces a feeling that there is much work to be
done before the body matches up to the standard shown in the
advertisements. A sense of physical self-disgust and hopelessness
can easily develop . . . these advertisements help to endorse the

powerful male attitude that women are passive bodies to be endlessly looked at, waiting to have their sexual attractiveness matched with *active* male sexual desire.

Source

J. Root (1984) *Pictures of Women: Sexuality*, Pandora, pp. 66–8.

References in Reading

J. Berger (1972) *Ways of Seeing*, Penguin/BBC.

R. Coward (1984) *Female Desire: Women's Sexuality Today*, Paladin.

K. Myers (1986) *Understains . . . The Sense and Seduction of Advertising*, Comedia.

Questions

1. Jane Root argues that advertisements reproduce sexism through the process of 'being-looked-at-ness'. How does this process operate?
2. What evidence does Kathy Myers provide to suggest that women are implicated in this process?
3. Why does Rosalind Coward argue that advertising encourages women to see their bodies as a project? What are likely to be the long-term effects of this?

☐ Challenging the Male Gaze

Deidre Pribram (1988) challenges the perspectives of John Berger and Jane Root who maintain that women are constantly, through the media, defined through the male gaze. She draws upon studies of film and music video to suggest that women are not passive victims of sexist representations by demonstrating that the intention of the text (film, advertisement, music video) may be used/read differently to the way it was intended.

Reading 2

Deidre Pribram (1988) asks how we come to perceive all forms of filmic gaze as male when women have taken up their proportionate share of seats in the cinema? How have we come to understand cinematic pleasure as pleasurable to the male viewer but not to the female? The camera was seen to represent only the male way of seeing and to construct the viewer as the 'gazer' who could only see through the eyes of men, leaving the female audience to identify with the male-as-subject or the female-as-object: what Laura Mulvey (1975) argues reproduces a structure of male looking/female to-be-looked-at-ness, which replicates the structure of unequal power relations between men and women, leaving women with no active spectatorial position at all. Jackie Stacey* argues that this gives women three frustrating options: masculinization, masochism or marginality.

It does not ask whether women actually take up a feminine and men a masculine spectator position. In the introduction to her book Pribram argues that an examination of female spectatorship involves three avenues: the individual female spectator, shaped by psychic and social processes of subject formation; female spectators as historically and socially constituted groups; and female audiences, participants in film's (and television's) broad popular base. She draws together the different contributions to this debate. From a study of film, Linda Williams argues that ideology is imposed repeatedly, in response to particular historical occurrences and changing spectatorial concerns. As such it can be understood more accurately as a *series* of varying strategies which attempt to keep dominant ideology dominant but must do so in response to continual challenges. Jeanne Allen's analysis suggests that a media product is amenable to more than a single reading, alternative interpretations are apparent within it. Christine Gledhill argues that ideology has to be continually negotiated because women's everyday experience and their history are important features that inform how they will receive ideology.

Jacqueline Bobo demonstrates how this (and black experience) enabled black women to construct alternative and favourable readings from *The Color Purple*. Using theories of cultural competency and articulation, she explains how social subjects can bring meaning to, or construct it from, a given text. Her analysis suggests that alternative ideologies are not necessarily embedded within cultural products but are equally embodied in cultural readings. Ann Kaplan takes this argument further. Drawing from her analysis of MTV she argues that music television offers the viewer a wide range of gazes and forms of address. The result is that television spectators – female and male – may make multiple identifications both within and across gender lines.

Source

E. D. Pribram (1988) 'Introduction', in E. D. Pribram (ed.) *Female Spectators: Looking at Film and Television*, Verso, pp. 1–11.

References in Reading

L. Mulvey (1975) 'Visual pleasure and narrative cinema', *Screen*, Vol. 16, No. 3, Autumn.

*Other references refer to articles in Pribram (1988) above.

Questions

1. Why does Jackie Stacey argue that only masculinization, masochism or marginality would be open to women if we accepted the theories of the 'gaze' theorists?
2. From the reading identify the ways that different theorists argue that ideology works.
3. How does Pribram's reading demonstrate that women are not duped by the ideological representation that they are given?

☐ Masculine Performance

The following readings examine how representations of men provide specific discourses – ways of speaking about – masculinity and frameworks for behaviour. Whilst appearance was seen to be a crucial feature of femininity, emphasis is placed upon the performance of the male. Richard Dyer (1983), argues, as Jane Root did, that such representations can lead to the long-term construction of anxieties.

Reading 3

In her book *The Male Nude* Walters traces the historical association of hardness with masculinity. She suggests that this hardness is phallic, not in the direct sense of being like an erect penis but rather in being symbolic of all that the phallus represents of 'abstract paternal power'. There is no doubt that the image of the phallus as power is widespread to the point of near universality, all the way from tribal and early Greek fertility symbols to the language of pornography, where the penis is endlessly described as a weapon, a tool, a source of terrifying power . . . The phallus is not just an arbitrarily chosen symbol of male power; it is crucial that the penis has provided the model for this symbol. Because only men have penises, phallic symbols, even if in some sense possessed by a woman (as may be the case with female rulers, for instance), are always symbols of ultimately male power. The woman who wields 'phallic' power does so in the interests of men.

This leads to the greatest instability of all for the male image. For the fact is that the penis isn't a patch on the phallus. The penis can never live up to the mystique implied by the phallus. Hence the excessive, even hysterical quality of so much male imagery. The clenched fists, the bulging muscles, the hardened jaw, the prolifera-tion of phallic symbols – they are all straining after what can hardly ever be achieved, the embodiment of the phallic mystique. This is even more the case with the male nude. The limp penis can never match up to the mystique that has kept it hidden from view for the last couple of centuries and even the erect penis looks awkward, stuck on to the man's body as if it is not part of him.

Like so much else about masculinity, images of men, founded upon such multiple instabilities, are such a strain. Looked at but pretending not to be, still yet asserting movement, phallic but weedy – there is seldom anything easy about such imagery. And the real trap .at the heart of these instabilities is that it is precisely *straining* that is held to be the great good, what makes a man a man. Whether head held high reaching up for an impossible transcend-ence or penis jerking up in a hopeless assertion of phallic mastery, men and women alike are asked to value the very things that make masculinity such an unsatisfactory definition of being human.

Source

R. Dyer (1983) 'Don't look now', in *Screen*, Vol. 23, No. 3/4, p. 206.

Questions

1. What does Richard Dyer suggest is the greatest instability for the male image?
2. Why does Richard Dyer argue that masculinity is such an unsatisfac-tory definition of being human?
3. Identify the differences between Richard Dyer's account of masculinity and Jane Root's (Reading 1) account of feminine representations.

□ Construction and Incorporation

The following is a commentary on what became known as the 'New Man' phenomenon: itself a media construction that attempted to frame our understanding of the changes in representations of masculinity. It shows how new ideas about masculinity were generated through an advertising campaign intent on opening new fashion markets. It demonstrates how anything 'new' has to be constructed in relation to the ideas that are already in place.

Reading 4

'Beware a Wolf in Sheep's Clothing' [a wool advertising campaign] came out about seven years ago:

> We wanted to persuade men to wear fashionable clothes, when fashion was thought effeminate. So we developed the idea of the urban animal – a guy on the prowl. Every once in a while you meet a man who exudes a threat, you accept that this guy is a little bit dangerous. We looked for models who were able to emit that threat, an image that other men would respect, and think, 'I wouldn't mind being him'. Yet he was wearing strong fashionable clothes. He was a loner who had no need for peer approval. It was a strategy to slowly persuade men into a new frame of mind regarding fashion.

As Rutherford (1988) comments on the advertising campaign the advertisement plays on men's resistance to, and adoption of, a more feminised image. For men to put their/our bodies on display contradicts the codes of who looks and who is looked at. It pacifies us. Men have held the power of the look, the symbolic owning of women's bodies. Reversing the gaze offers the symbol of men's bodies on offer to women. The model in this advertisement snarls his unease and disapproval, caught in a feminised image that strips him of his masculine power. His snarl, and the title of the advertisement, both warn the viewer (woman) that he still retains that animal predatory sexuality that is proof of his manhood. It is an image that confronts the insecurities of a masculine identity in doubt. The model disavows his passivity through his aggressive look, through demonstrating that he still has control over definitions of who he is.

Source

J. Rutherford (1988) 'Who's that man', in R. Chapman and J. Rutherford (eds) *Male Order: Unwrapping Masculinity*, Lawrence & Wishart, p. 32.

Questions

1. Why does Rutherford argue that it is difficult to put men's bodies on display in advertising?
2. How does Rutherford demonstrate how the media are involved in constructing limits and boundaries around the way we speak of masculinity?
3. How does Rutherford show how the media are involved in constructing 'consent' to new images in their attempt to sell things?

☐ Racist Media

The next reading suggests that the British media is undoubtedly racist. It argues that racist reporting and representations legitimate racism. It also demonstrates how the media are able to close down and delegitimate any attempts that are made to challenge racism and inequality.

Reading 5

The main way in which black people are treated in newspapers is as a social problem. Black people are portrayed as constituting a threat to white British society, first through their immigration to this country and then, when settled here, as posing a law and order problem. This is done in a number of ways: through dramatic presentation of stories involving banner headlines and prominent positioning, provocative or damning quotations and statements from people portrayed as authoritative figures, popular stereotypes, repetition of unreliable stories, and the creation and manipulation of popular fears. Increasingly, the press in Britain (with a few exceptions) has taken an active role in legitimating racism by promoting racist ideas and by attacking attempts to tackle racism.

In the daily reporting of news with a race dimension, long-standing assumptions, myths and stereotypes are regularly reproduced. Recent years have seen a proliferation of press commentators for whom race issues are an urgent and recurrent concern. These include writers such as Andrew Alexander in the *Daily Mail*, George Gale in the *Daily Express*, Ray Mills in the *Daily Star* and John Vincent in *The Sun*.

These writers represent many different styles – from elevated reflections aimed at shifting perceptions to populist rhetoric demanding and encouraging action. In content, though, they have concentrated on a set of common themes and promoted a narrow range of broadly similar perspectives. In particular, they have supported and justified policies which restrict the entry of black people into Britain; they have questioned the notion of a multiracial society; they have challenged established definitions of racism; and they have offered their own portrayals of different minority groups . . . It can be argued that their contributions on race issues have reinforced racist analyses, myths and stereotypes and undermined anti-racism.

In such coverage, the press has created and fostered a climate of fear in which white people are portrayed as the victims of anti-racist madness and vindictiveness. The anti-racists are the 'thought police', the 'dictators', the proponents of a new form of apartheid and it is the white people who lose out from equal opportunities and multiracial education policies.

What such papers do is to deny, against all the evidence, that racism and systematic racial discrimination, exist in Britain . . . Black people are only presented in a positive way when they share the values of particular newspapers. In particular, they should not talk about racism or discrimination; they should not hold on to any kind of minority culture or religion; and they should value personal and financial success above most other things.

Source

P. Gordon and D. Rosenberg (1989) *Daily Racism: The Press and Black People in Britain*, The Runnymede Trust, pp. 3, 23–5, 50–1, 57.

Questions

1. How are black people portrayed by the British media?
2. How have certain press reporters been able to turn the issue of racism into one in which white people are portrayed as victims? How is this likely to affect the responses of white people, who have no knowledge or experience of black people?
3. Gordon and Rosenberg argue that such press coverage makes racism against black people invisible. How does this contribute to the reproduction of racism in general?

☐ 'Sheep's Eye Burgers'

Jenkins (1990) describes how the media's portrayal of Arabs constructs them as the 'other'. This technique enables the reader to construct their difference and distance from that which is not 'normal'. It also shows how fear is invoked in racist descriptions. It points out the historical consistency in the reproduction of racism against Arabs.

Reading 6

According to a newspaper cutting in front of me, Saddam Hussein 'has imported a £50,000 custom built Lambourghini sports car from Italy'. The writer claims that 'in Baghdad, there are already mutterings over the President's lavish spending on clothes and the purchase, ostensibly for state use, of a well-appointed Danish built yacht.' Saddam, it concludes is 'in serious danger of being removed' . . . The date of the cutting is 12th January 1983. The author is that distinguished Arabist, Nigel Dempster. Quite apart from his flawed powers of prediction, poor old Dempster has clearly picked the wrong stereotype. There are only three basic Arab characters in British journalism: the savage, the terrorist, and the spendthrift. Saddam is evidently a savage, not a spendthrift. The savage is probably the most enduring of the three anyway. Consider another item from my files – a cartoon by the *Daily Express*'s Cummings. It refers to the discovery of the Libyan connection in the miners' strike, and shows a Kinnock-faced rat deserting a Scargill-faced ship. The latter is saying, 'Surely you're not leaving – just when Colonel Kadhafi is serving camel-en-casserole and sheep's eyes on toast in the first class lounge.' (Camels and sheep's eyes are recurring motifs in this sort of thing.) Cumming's cartoon of the Camp David summit was equally subtle. Swarthy Arabs are shown holding drawings of Begin embracing Sadat, Sadat kissing Begin and Begin holding Sadat's hand. The caption: 'Feelthy pictures . . . feelthy pictures.'

Anti-Arabism has never been taboo in the same way as, say, anti-Semitism (or anti-Germanism). Perhaps because it's so unthinkable, it has occasionally got British companies in trouble. Dunlop once ran an advertisement showing a wild-eyed Arab brandishing a scimitar from behind a tyre. The copy read: "The Dunlop Elite saves 5p a gallon (As tested by the RAC. And thoroughly detested by oilmen.)". There was an outcry throughout the Arab world. Dunlop was forced to apologise and fire its ad agency, Saatchi and Saatchi.

These attitudes are remarkably persistent. A few years ago, *The Sun* printed a front-page story which claimed that an unmarried air hostess had been forced to flee the Middle East with her new-born baby to avoid being flung in an 'Arab jail'. This was almost entirely invention. But when a complaint was lodged with *The Sun*, the newspaper didn't seek to claim that the story was true: instead, it justified it on the grounds that 'what we printed coincided with accepted views about the differences between Middle Eastern and western social attitudes.' In other words, the existence of a stereotype was sufficient reason for its perpetuation.

The oil crisis of 1973 provoked a sustained bout of anti-Arabism in Britain, mostly of the 'Arab as spendthrift' variety. With the Arab world in turmoil we may be in for another burst. It is not just the tabloids that are guilty. In *The Independent on Sunday* this week, the Palestinian critic Edward Said deplored the shallowness of western attitudes to Arab culture. A few pages away, the same 'quality' newspaper ran a cartoon. Its title *Jane's Aggressive Camels*. And on Tuesday, *The Independent* cartoon showed a US field kitchen serving up 'sheep's eye burgers'. Ha bloody ha.

Source

J. Jenkins (1990) 'Taking liberties', *New Statesman and Society*, 17.8.90, p. 7.

Questions

1. How does Jenkins show that the categories 'other' and 'normal' are used to construct frameworks for the understanding of Arab peoples?
2. How do the examples cited legitimate racism?
3. Where, in the media, are we likely to find representations that could challenge racism?

☐ Transgression

Just as black people and Arabs are constructed as a problem by the media so is the category 'youth'. However, young people are able to utilise this categorisation to make the transition into adulthood. Hebdige (1988) in the following reading, examines how this coding of young people frames the responses they are able to make. They make use of their 'problem' status in order to be heard.

Reading 7

I shall begin with a proposition – one that is so commonplace that its significance is often overlooked – that in our society, youth is present only when its presence is a problem, or is regarded as a problem. Since the 1950s, the 'politics of youth' in this country has been played out, first and foremost as spectacle: as the politics of photogenic confrontations, of consumption and 'life style'. More precisely, the category 'youth' gets mobilised in official documentary discourse in concerned or outraged editorials and features, at those times when young people make their presence felt by going 'out of bounds' by resisting through rituals, dressing strangely, striking bizarre attitudes, breaking rules, breaking bottles, windows, heads, issuing rhetorical challenges to the law.

When young people do these things, when they adopt these strategies, they get talked about, taken seriously, their grievances are acted upon. They get arrested, harassed, admonished, disciplined, incarcerated, applauded, vilified, emulated, listened to. They get defended by social workers and other concerned philanthropists. They get explained by sociologists, social psychologists, by pundits of every political complexion. In other words, there is a logic to transgression.

When disaffected adolescents from the inner city, more particularly when disaffected inner city *unemployed* adolescents resort to symbolic and actual violence, they are playing with the only power at their disposal: the power to discomfit. The power, that is, to pose – to pose a threat. Far from abandoning good sense, they are acting in accordance with a logic which is manifest – that as a condition of their entry into the adult domain, the field of public debate, the place where real things really happen, they must first challenge the symbolic order which guarantees their subordination by nominating them 'children', 'youngsters', 'young folk', 'kids'.

Source

D. Hebdige (1988) *Hiding in the Light*, Comedia/Routledge, pp. 17–35.

Questions

1. Why should youth only be present in the media when they are a problem?
2. How does the media construct the category of youth?
3. Other than making their presence felt, how would young people get access to the media in order to represent their ideas and views?

☐ Coronation Street

The 'North' is used by the media to construct a particularly romantic notion of the working class. This construction evokes a sense of unity which enables any inequalities to be hidden. It provides an example of how a mythical and nostalgic past is used in the context of a supposedly real context to appear as authentic.

Reading 8

Coronation Street provides the representation of a permanent urban working class. It is founded upon peoples' knowledge of past events, or, in the case of younger viewers, conceptions and beliefs about what such times were like. From a period of industrial greatness and prosperity the North withstood the break up of its communities, the loss of major industries, the fragmentation of extended family relationships, and the declining of its particular cultural practices, traditions, customs and behaviour. Simultaneously the mass media expanded rapidly, cities grew and townships extended as workers migrated into areas of employment.

In Salford, the model for Coronation Street, the close affinity with the environment was shattered with the demolition of rows of terraced back-to-back houses, and erection of high rise dwellings. Such communal reorganisation is directly responsible for the 'idealisation' of the North through the need to reconstruct cultural identity. This reconstruction may appear in the following (though not mutually exclusive) forms:

i) *Direct*   — dealing with historical elements (actuality)
                 — set in the past (fictional)
ii) *Indirect*   — or contemporary
                 — set in the present yet not exactly true to life
                 — a mirror of the past (popular memory of

'good old days')
- life as it is lived (for some)
- life as it could/should by lived

iii) *Additional*:   Can be Direct or Indirect PLUS,
i.e. the use of comedy for effect
- tongue-in-cheek, clichés, exaggerated caricatures
made from stereotypes
- more blatant, e.g. *Brass*

Whichever form or forms the representation takes certain images constantly recur, becoming 'fixed' indices of Northerness. The flat cap, braces, apron, rollers, black pudding and clogs are merely a few items from a very long list symbolising Working-classness/ Northerness, or Masculinity/Northerness. Particular characteristics reappear, recognisable 'types' exist within and between programmes, contributing to the audiences' expectations and reading.

The success of Coronation Street has made more socially (and academically) respectable the widespread myth that somewhere out there, remote from the metropolis and yet thereby nearer to the heart of England, is a society where blunt common sense and unsentimental affection raises people above the concerns of industrialisation, or unions, or politics.

Source

E. Adams (1985) *Television and 'The North'*. Working Paper in Cultural Studies, Birmingham. Centre for Contemporary Cultural Studies, pp. 46–7, 49.

Questions

1. Describe a typical 'Northerner'. Where do you think your images come from?
2. Why does the media equate northenness and community with the working class? Can you think of any other ways that the working class could be represented?
3. If people have no experience or knowledge of the North and/or working class, what frameworks for understanding behaviour is Coronation Street likely to provide?

General Questions

1. 'Sexism is a most notable feature of nearly all the output of the mass media.' (T. Marks, *Sex and Gender*). Discuss this statement in the light of sociological evidence. (*AEB 1982*)

2. How does the media contribute to the construction of 'common sense' understandings of what is 'natural' and what is 'normal'? Use the readings to provide examples for your answer.
3. How does the media both sell commodities and win consent for social order through specific representations?
4. 'The mass media may not tell us what to think, but they do tell us what to think about.' Explain and discuss. (*AEB 1986*)

Further Reading

R. Chapman, J. Rutherford (eds) (1988) *Male Order: Unwrapping Masculinity*, Lawrence and Wishart.

R. Coward (1984) *Female Desire: Women's Sexuality Today*, Paladin Books.

C. Critcher, M. Parker and R. Sondhi (1975) *Race in the Provincial Press: A case study of five West Midlands newspapers*. Prepared for the Division of Applied Social Science, UNESCO. Birmingham. Centre for Contemporary Cultural Studies.

K. Davies, J. Dickey and T. Stratford (eds) (1987) *Out of Focus: Writing on Women and the Media*, The Women's Press.

L. Gamman and M. Marshment (eds) (1988) *The Female Gaze: Women as Viewers of Popular Culture*, The Women's Press.

J. Lull (ed.) (1988) *World Families Watch Television*, Sage.

A. McRobbie (ed.) (1989) *Zoot Suits and Second-hand Dresses. An Anthology of Fashion and Music*, Macmillan.

S. Redhead (1990) *The End-of-the-Century Party. Youth and Pop Towards 2000,* Manchester University Press.

J. Root (1984) *Pictures of Women*, Pandora Press.

5 | Influence and effects of the media

The media construct 'reality'. In discussing gender, race, class and age, we have examined the complex processes by which we are persuaded to accept these constructions. That the media do influence events, issues and ideas, that they do affect the way we behave, might seem beyond doubt. Yet, an historical survey of media effects research suggests that there has been very little agreement as to the extent and kinds of effects the media have, or as to how these effects occur.

This is partly to do with the nature of research itself, which can never be conceived, designed or undertaken in isolation from its social, political and ideological context. In the sense that all research is motivated, it should be seen as a mechanism of social control. This is not to suggest that researchers already 'know' the answers to questions they ask, but to acknowledge that 'research' is a powerful discourse informed by and circulating amongst other discourses. In discussing the effects and influence of the media, we are discussing the processes by which social meanings are created and sustained.

We should not be surprised, then, that attitudes towards media effects have differed over time. McQuail (1987, Reading 1) talks of a 'natural history' of thought concerning media effects, veering between research which argued that the media were all-powerful, and that which argued that the media have no or only minimal effect.

Earliest attitudes towards the media, influenced by deep-rooted cultural suspicion of all popular culture, reflected the view that the press, cinema and radio were able to shape opinion and mould behaviour almost at will. The massive popularity of these media in the 1930s led conservatives to talk of cultural debasement, and Marxists to develop the thesis that the masses were being injected with a repressive ideology. This 'hypodermic syringe' model of media effects proved remarkably influential, despite research undertaken from the 1930s to the 1960s which stressed that the media operate within complex structures of social relationships, so that direct media influence is unlikely or impossible. At its extreme, it was argued that these other social and cultural factors were so powerful in influencing opinions and behaviour, that media effects were negligible.

The popularity of television from the 1960s onwards coincided with a return to the concept of a powerful and influential media. In particular, a significant contribution came from those cultural affects theorists who shifted attention away from the media's immediate influence on short-term attitudes and behaviour, towards their role in constructing longer-term structures of belief. For many, the media have been seen as a powerful means of legitimating control by positioning us to accept certain ideological constructions. As we have already seen in Chapter 4, the ubiquitous and reiterative nature of specific representations of gender and race have the long-term effect of rendering them 'natural', the product, apparently, of our 'common sense'.

Whilst this view of the media is one which informs much of this book, we are not arguing that people are merely the passive dupes of a sustained ideological campaign which ensures their subordination. As we maintain in the following chapter, people make use of the media for their own purposes and are capable of opposing and 'resisting' intended meanings. The construction of meaning occurs through the interaction between media texts and their readers who are, as Morley (1986) reminds us, socially situated. However, it is clear that the media do have their effects, and some of these are apparent almost immediately. The weather forecast will influence the clothes we wear, an advertising campaign can change our spending patterns, we telephone to donate money to charity during a telethon. In more complex ways, our personal behaviour may change as a response to watching programmes about violent crime in the cities, or we may decide not to allow our children to watch certain television programmes. Advertising campaigns, party political broadcasts, cinema and video rental classification, anti-pornography campaigns, the establishment of regulatory watchdogs such as the Broadcasting Standards Council, all recognise that the media have an effect.

References

D. Morley (1986) *Family Television: Cultural Power and Domestic Leisure*, Comedia.

□ Levels and Kinds of Media Effect

This general acceptance that the media do have effects of various kinds, and the equally general disagreement as to what these are and how they occur, is reflected in the complexity of the concepts and terminology involved in media effects research methodology.

Reading 1

In speaking of 'media effects' we are necessarily referring to what has already occurred as a direct consequence of mass communication, whether intended or not. The expression 'media power', on the other hand, refers to a potential for the future or a statement of probability about effects, under given conditions. 'Media effectiveness' is a statement about the efficiency of media in achieving a given aim and can apply to past, present or future, but always implying intention. Such distinctions can often be important for precision of speaking about the media, although it is hard to keep to a consistent usage. Even more essential for research and theory is to observe the distinction between 'level' of occurrence, distinguishing at least the levels of: individual; group or organization; social institution; whole society; and culture. Each or all can be affected by mass communication and effects at one level always implies effects at other levels. It happens that most research has been carried out at the individual level, with consequent difficulties for drawing conclusions about effects at collective or higher levels, as recommended in the current research phase.

Perhaps the most confusing aspects of research on effects is the multiplicity and complexity of the phenomena involved. Broad distinctions are normally made between: effects which are cognitive (to do with knowledge and opinion); those which are affectual (relating to attitude and feelings); effects on behaviour. These distinctions have been treated in early research as distinct and following a logical order ... In fact it is no longer found easy to sustain the distinction between the three concepts ... To add to the complexity, much of our evidence comes from replies to questionnaires which are themselves individual acts of verbal behaviour from which we hope to reconstruct collective phenomena, often with an inextricable mixture of cognitive and affectual elements.

A final word should be said at this point about another kind of differentiation – that of type and direction of effect. Klapper (1960) distinguished between 'conversion', 'minor change' and 'reinforcement' – respectively: change according to the intention of the communicator; change in form or intensity; confirmation by the receiver of his or her own existing beliefs and opinions. This three-fold distinction needs to be widened to include other possibilities, especially at the supra-individual level, leading to the following: Media may

- cause intended change (conversion)
- cause unintended change
- cause minor change (form or intensity)
- facilitate change (intended or not)
- reinforce what exists (no change)
- prevent change

The categories are mainly self-explanatory, but the facilitation of change refers to the mediating role of media in wider processes of change in society. Both of the last two named imply no effect, but involve different conceptions of media working. Reinforcement is an observable consequence of selective attention by the receiver to content which is congruent with existing views, aided perhaps by a generous supply of such content.

The second, 'preventing change', implies deliberate supply of one-sided or ideologically shaped content in order to inhibit change in a conforming public. The 'no change' effect from the media, of which we have so much evidence, requires very close attention because of its long-term consequences. It is indeed a somewhat misleading expression, since anything that alters the probability of opinion or belief distribution in the future is an intervention into social process and thus an effect.

Source

D. McQuail (1987) *Mass Communication Theory: An Introduction*, 2nd edn, Sage, pp. 256–7.

Reference in Reading

J. Klapper (1960) *The Effect of Mass Communication*, Free Press.

Questions

1. What actual examples can you suggest to illustrate the difference between 'media effects', 'media power' and 'media effectiveness'?
2. What methodological problems in researching media influence and effects does McQuail identify? Why are they a problem?
3. How useful is Klapper's taxonomy? How might researchers begin to gauge the different levels and kinds of effect?

☐ Children and Television Violence

Early studies of media effects concentrated on young people and the cinema in the USA in the late 1920s. The most famous, established by the Payne Fund in 1928, tried to examine the relationship between film-watching and juvenile crime. Although they failed to establish direct causal links, such studies did little to dispel cultural myths about the ability of the media to deprave the audience. Whatever the limitations of the 'hypodermic syringe' model of media effects, the belief that the media have direct, immediate and damaging effects on people gained ground with the widespread introduction of television in the 1960s.

Reading 2

A report recently appeared in my local newspaper, the Exeter *Express and Echo*, under the headline GANG COPIES A TELEVI-SION IDEA ON A BURGLARY. Apparently the burglars used a method of cutting window glass they had seen on the television series *Dixon of Dock Green*. They received prison sentences of up to three years, and one of them asked for sixty-five other offences to be taken into consideration. The judge commented that their crimes provided 'yet another example to television producers of the undesirability of exhibiting methods of committing crimes'.

The mass media have long provided convenient scapegoats for the most glaring of society's ills, and the visual communications systems have been especially popular as objects of blame. As early as 1916 a Parisian gentleman drew up an indictment of the cinema, which he claimed was 'a propagator of vice and crime', and over the years both cinema and television have frequently been charged with providing the breeding grounds for all kinds of social disturbance.

Numerous horror stories have been quoted in the press and elsewhere, bearing witness to the apparently evil effects of the television medium. The book produced in 1961 to describe the major survey by Schramm, Lyle and Parker, reported a number of such tales. One described the arrest of a 16-year-old boy who had been seen entering the cellar of a house. The boy was wearing gloves and he claimed that he had learned to do so from television shows he had seen, in order not to leave fingerprints. Another account concerned a boy aged nine. After showing his father a highly critical school report card the boy proposed improving the situation by giving the teacher a Christmas present of a box of poisoned sweets. He explained that this technique had been demonstrated on the previous week's television, being used by a man who had decided to kill his wife . . .

Such stories are by no means uncommon. Whether or not they amount to real evidence that television has caused children to indulge in anti-social behaviour, as well as influencing the form of anti-social acts, the manner in which they are typically reported in the press indicates a strong belief that television is to blame.

Source

M. J. A. Howe (1977) *Television and Children*, New University Education, pp. 71–2.

Reference in Reading

W. Schram, J. Lyle and E. Parker (1961) *Television in the Lives of our Children*, Stanford University Press.

Questions

1. Why might cinema and television in particular been seen as 'popular objects of blame' for producing anti-social attitudes and behaviour?
2. Why should such 'evidence' of causal links between television and delinquent behaviour be so readily accepted by so many people?
3. Why has so much research into the effects of television on young people concentrated on negative effects, and largely ignored any positive influences the medium has?

□ Broadcasting, Sex and Violence

Although researchers such as Halloran (1970) pointed out the complexity of identifying and attributing media effects, the hypodermic syringe mentality still informs much of the debate about the media, particularly where representations of sex and violence are concerned. It also has an influence on contemporary media and broadcasting policy. In the next reading, two short extracts illustrate this.

Reference

J. Halloran (1970) *The Effects of Television*, Granada.

Reading 3

A

... the Government has sought to strengthen standards and rein-force the work of the individual regulatory bodies by establishing a Broadcasting Standards Council (BSC), initially on a non-statutory basis. The Government announced on 16 May 1988 that Lord Rees-Mogg would be the first Chairman of the BSC.

During the pre-statutory phase the Council's role is to:

- draw up, in consultation with the broadcasting authorities and other responsible bodies in the broadcasting, cable and video fields, a code on the portrayal of sex and violence and standards of taste and decency;
- monitor and report on the portrayal of violence and sex, and standards of taste and decency, in television and radio program-mes received in the UK and in video works;
- receive, consider and make findings on complaints and com-ments from individuals and organisations on matters within its competence and ensure that such findings are effectively publi-cised;
- undertake research on such matters as the nature and effects on attitudes and behaviour in the portrayal of violence and sex in television and radio programmes and in video works;
- prepare an annual report, which the Home Secretary will lay before Parliament and publish.

Source

Home Office (1988) *Broadcasting In the '90s: Competition, Choice and Quallity*, White Paper on Broadcasting, HMSO.

B Cable code on violent videos

■ by Quentin Smith

THE CABLE Authority is to draw up a code of practice governing the portrayal of sex and violence in pop videos.

The rise in the number of channels showing pop videos has prompted the authority to take action.

"We want to control the screening of anti-social and potentially harmful acts," said director of programming Tony Currie.

"We are concerned that the portrayal of some acts may lead to imitation by young people, such as smoking cigarettes, taking drugs, and promiscuous sex, which could lead to AIDS," he said.

The Cable Authority was among the broadcasting bodies which outlawed the controversial video which accompanied singer George Michael's hit *I Want Your Sex*.

The authority has also recommended that some videos be aired "late in the evening", when they are unlikely to be seen by younger viewers.

Currie said the authority decided to take action after it was approached by music channels for advice on the screening of pop videos.

"Instead of giving individual guidance on individual videos it seems more sensible to draw up a code and let programmers decide what is suitable and when it should be shown," said Currie.

The authority expects to publish the code of conduct by the end of the year.

Figure 5.1 (Source: *Broadcast*, 14.4.89, p. 4).

Questions

1. What justification is there for the Broadcasting Standards Council's (BSC's) narrow remit to monitor representations of sex and violence?
2. The BSC's brief places emphasis on publishing its findings. Is this motivated solely by a desire to inform, or should we regard it as an attempt at social control through agenda-setting?
3. What attitude towards media effects informs the article on pop videos? Is there research evidence to support these attitudes?

☐ How Television Affects the Citizen's Political Outlook

From the 1950s onwards, media effects research increasingly emphasised that the relationship between media and audiences was more complex than that implied by the 'hypodermic' model. Katz and Lazarsfeld (1960) stressed that people lived in groups, and that groups, and opinion leaders within groups, were important in the formation of social attitudes. Arguing that the power of the media had been exaggerated, they suggested that people did not really respond actively to information given through the media, even in news and current affairs material which presented relevant social and political information. This approach informed much of the research undertaken in the 1960s and 1970s into the influence of television and election campaigns on political opinion.

Reference

E. Katz and P. F. Lazarsfeld (1960) *Personal Influence*, Free Press.

Reading 4

Interpretations of TV's political power over individual viewers have often reflected shifting fashions of intellectual climate and mood. In fact, three waves of opinion have more or less succeeded each other. The political influence of television was initially magnified, subsequently minimized and now – we are unsure!

There was certainly a time when the political impact of television was conceived in rather dramatic terms. The popularity of the medium, its visual dimension, and its domestic setting – all inspired vivid impressions of TV's potential for jolting viewers out of their settled political grooves.

But then a mood of reaction set in, and much attention was focussed on the strength of electoral resistance to persuasion. In Britain the first fruits of research were experienced as a douche of cold water. During the General Election of 1959, Joseph Trenaman and Denis McQuail surveyed the political opinions and media exposure of a sample of electors, who were interviewed before and after the campaign. Although they detected a campaign of swing of attitudes in favour of the Conservative Party, they reported that the political viewing engaged in by the sampled voters had made no difference at all to the outcome. In the words of Trenaman and McQuail (1961), 'political change was neither related to the degree of exposure nor to any particular programme or argument put forward by the parties'. Following the emergence of similar results from a series of surveys in other countries, a veritable law of the impotence of all mass media (including the press and radio as well as TV) was eventually formulated. This was supported by an ingenious explanation, which purported to show why neither floating voters nor more stable electors were persuasible by mass communications.

On the face of it, floating voters – electors who are willing to switch from one party to another – should be open to influence. But because many of them have only a faint interest in politics, they tend to pay but a cursory attention to political affairs through the mass media. Consequently, they were said to be shielded from media influence by their own apathy and indifference. What about the rest of the electorate? When following a campaign, they were said to look mainly for messages emanating from their own favoured candidates and parties. Thus, they were also protected from media influence – by their tendency to engage in what sociologists called 'selective exposure'. Even if they happened to receive propaganda from some alien political source, they would usually interpret it in the light of their existing opinions and loyalties. For all these reasons it was concluded that a political campaign mounted through the mass media usually 'reinforces more than it converts'.

Source

Jay G. Blumler (1970) 'The political effects of television', in J. Halloran (ed.), *The Effects of Television*, Panther, pp. 74–6.

Reference in Reading

J. S. M. Trenaman and D. McQuail (1961) *Television and the Political Image*, Methuen.

Questions

1. Blumler talks of 'shifting fashions of intellectual climate and mood'. What does he mean by this and how do such shifts in attitude take place?
2. What reasons are given for the apparent unimportance of the media in affecting political attitudes? What other factors might influence the formation of such attitudes?
3. Since the late 1960s, it has been argued that TV campaigns have been increasingly influential in elections both in the UK and USA. What evidence exists to support this view?

☐ Television News in the United States

The view that people make selective use of the media on the basis of their own perceived social needs came to be known as the 'uses and gratifications' approach to media effects. We shall say more about ways in which people use the media in the following chapter. However, in the remaining readings for this chapter, we examine the power of the media to construct social agendas and attitudes, especially through the news. Between them, ITV's *News At Ten* and the BBC's *Nine O'Clock News* regularly attract audiences in excess of 16 million. In the USA, audiences are even larger, suggesting that news is both popular and influential.

Reading 5

Americans like news. Every day 65 million Americans watch the news on one of the three major television networks. Even more viewers watch an additional half-hour or more of local TV news, produced by nearly 600 stations affiliated with the networks and a number of other independent stations. Surveys show TV news to be the dominant source of mass information in our society, and people believe it to be more credible than any other media. The growth and influence of news channels may be the most important – but least understood – of our technological accomplishments. Philip Elliott (1972) notes how the organization behind these channels enables a few people to define what is significant for us all:

> In news bulletins, information about people and events in society comes filtered through the selection and presentation decisions made by television newsmen. Their ideas on what makes news decide which people and issues will receive publicity through the medium.

This is important since we run our lives according to pictures in our head. As long as many of these images come from TV news, then the work of transforming events into news is an act of power that touches us all. My research leads me to conclude that news messages have played a significant part in our history and will continue to help shape our future. I think that these messages have a far greater impact than the events they are claimed to reflect. This is why all facets of the news process and news perspective must be understood.

One reason Americans like TV news is that we depend on it. The size and complexity of our cities and country prohibit first-hand experience with many events that influence us. This is especially true in a technological society, where a decision thousands of miles away can affect our personal lives. But technology and size are not the only considerations.

Our society is not an observable thing like a collectivity of shared values and goals. It is a collage of different and often conflicting ethnic and racial groups, religious affiliations, occupational interests, age and sex divisions, and geographical peculiarities. Indeed, it is still an open question whether or not the people living within our borders even constitute a single society. Such diversity does not promote shared experience and understanding. This seething pluralism, plus the vast numbers and daily routines of Americans, makes shared knowledge and interests – the foundation of any social order – difficult to attain. This is why we must understand TV news: it is one of the few things we have in common.

Another reason Americans like news is its availability and meaning. The growth of the news business, and especially the advent of television in the last three decades, have led us to expect to know about major events. The coverage of political conventions, state funerals, and spectacular disasters are noteworthy in anyone's book. They are news because they have practical and emotional significance for most people. Though there are few events of this magnitude, the meaning of news is infused with such examples. This is why people tend to equate media presentations with significance; if something is in (on) the news, then it *must* be important.

Source

David L. Altheide (1974) *Creating Reality: How TV News Distorts Events*, Sage, pp. 11–12.

Reference in Reading

P. Elliott (1972) *The Making of a Television Series – a Case Study in the Production of Culture*, Constable.

Questions

1. Research does show that people regard news on TV as being more credible than in the other media. Why might this be?
2. Why does the writer suggest that the ability to translate events into news represents 'an act of power'?
3. What problems are involved in the argument that TV news is important because it encourages social consensus?

□ Acid House

The power to establish a social agenda through selection of issues and events deemed significant is not unique to television. In an important study, Cohen (1989) noted the role of the British press in establishing a dominant discourse through which social problems are identified and articulated, often beyond their real significance. He noted how the newspapers exaggerated the importance of some rather minor seaside fights betwen young people – 'folk devils' – so that they appeared as a major threat to established social order and values. This process of amplification, the creation of what Cohen termed 'moral panics', remains an important aspect of media power.

Reading 6

The summer was over when on October 1, *The Sun* signalled the dawn of Acid House as 'cool and groovy'. Then, just as swiftly, the paper took an about turn and captained an offensive of 'panic' proportions, indicated by headlines like: EVIL OF ECSTASY (*The Sun*, October 19); BAN THIS KILLER MUSIC (*Daily Post*, October 24); ACID HOUSE HORROR (*The Sun*, October 25); DRUG CRAZED ACID HOUSE FANS (*The Sun*, October 28); *GIRL 21 DROPS DEAD AT ACID DISCO (The Sun*, October 31); ACID KIDS LURED TO HOLLAND (*Daily Mirror*, November 14).

A chorus of celebrities was called to comment on the state of the nation's youth. Sir Alistair Burnet gravely presented the television crew 'evidence' of drug abuse at illegal warehouse parties, only to find his *News at Ten* broadcast inevitably sampled on a record, echoing the Renegade Sound Wave's earlier use of the programme's theme music and Big Ben chimes. Jonathan King preferred to call it 'rubbish' Peter Powell, a Radio 1 disc jockey, thought it 'the closest thing to zombiedom'. Matt Goss, from teen stars Bros, told of his mate who had been to an Acid House club, where everybody was 'out of their heads', and sensible Rick Astley astutely noted that 'they may as well call it heroin house'. Indeed, the media account they referred to was one of 'chilling' dimensions: a tabloid version of the bogeyman, steeped in the familiar language of the horror story. Acid Pied Pipers, the 'Mister Bigs' of Acid House – unscrupulous drug dealers and warehouse party organizers – were witnessed in a seduction of the innocent. Magical bogeymen tempted their unsuspecting prey with their evil wares: Ecstasy, Acid, 'Killer Music' that cast its alluring spell. Smiley, here, became a sinister calling card with hypnotic properties, as the unfortunate were sucked into the 'hellish nightmare'.

The potential victims in this tale of an evil cult, which the tabloids recounted, promptly materialized, as the generalities of 'youths', 'teenagers' and 'schoolchildren' gave way to specifically gendered subjects. *The Sun* on November 7 told how '14 year old Jenny' swallowed Ecstasy for the first time. *Daily Mirror* on the same day explained the way in which a 'young girl rolled a joint of cannabis' and how 'three young girls were spotted taking the mind-blowing drug LSD', and, further, quoted one 17 year old claiming 'I had some Acid in me'. This portrayal of the typical Acid House victim as a young woman culminated in *The Sun* headline on November 24, ACID FIENDS SPIKE PAGE 3 GIRL'S DRINK. It was reported how Spanish men who were spiking girls' drinks 'would lie in wait and rape them'. In this case, the greatest danger of sexual violation – previously implied in the talk of sex orgies, outrageous romps and use of the 'sex drug' Ecstasy at Acid House parties – was made explicit. Women were thus established as the victims of deviance within the Acid House scene.

Source

S. Redhead (1990) *The End of the Century Party: Youth and Pop Towards 2000*, University of Manchester Press, pp. 2–3.

Reference in Reading

S. Cohen (1989) *Folk Devils and Moral Panics*, Blackwell.

Questions

1. (a) **Who or what are the 'folk devils' here and what is the threat they are said to represent?**

(b) What 'folk devils' are currently portrayed by the media and what threat are they said to represent?
2. In what ways do the media position audiences against the groups that are the object of attack?
3. What other examples of 'panics' have there been? How successfully have they influenced public attitudes, opinion and behaviour?

☐ News and the Limits of Political Imagination

The previous reading suggested that the media do have the power to influence public attitude towards particular issues and events. A great deal of current research is interested in the role of news as hegemonic agent, as an important mechanism in gaining our consent to the social system. Jensen (1986, 1990), in his studies of American news, attempts to relate the possibility of reader 'resistance' to the undeniable power of institutional media to set agendas and limit conceptual frameworks. Through a series of interviews and questionnaires, he establishes that people make use of television news for a wide range of purposes, but comes to some important conclusions.

Reading 7

Whereas a range of diversional and contextual uses are attributed to American television news, the respondents place a particular emphasis on the traditional political relevances of news. The interviews serve to identify a contradiction in the audience definition of 'political relevance'. Even though the concrete information of events and issues is characterized as, in principle, a resource for political participation and action, the respondents suggest that the central relevance of news be thought of in terms of *legitimation*. Television news provides a daily forum for the viewers' reassertion of their political competence within a representative form of democracy, but it is not conceived of as a point of departure for action in the institutions and organizations of political life. The contradictory nature of news reception bears witness, in a wider perspective, to a divided form of everyday consciousness which derives from contradictions at the macrolevel of social organization. On the one hand, the news media are potentially a tool for political influence and change; on the other hand, such social uses of news by the audience–public are not institutionalized and do not have a precedent in practical politics. It is a contradictory *social* definition of news which manifests itself at the level of media use and experience.

The interviews further suggest that, at least with respect to the social uses of news, the differences between socioeconomic groups may be negligible. While earlier research shows that there are major differences between such groups in terms of media consumption as well as their decoding of specific texts, it is plausible that viewer-citizens generally are constrained in their uses of news by the dominant social definition and institutional framework of politics. The reception of television news may, accordingly, be seen as an agent of *hegemony* which serves to reassert the limits of the political imagination. As the theoretical literature on hegemony argues, even though the social production of meaning can be seen as a process in which the prevailing definition of reality may be challenged and revised, the outcome of that process is overdetermined by the historical and institutional framework of communication. The polysemy of media texts is only a political potential, and the oppositional decoding of media is not yet a manifestation of political power. As Marx notes, 'men make their own history, but they do not make it just as they please'. Similarly, people make their own sense of the media, but that sense is bounded by the social definition of genres.

Source

K. B. Jensen (1990) 'The politics of polysemy: television news, everyday consciousness and political action', in *Media, Culture and Society*, Vol. 12, pp. 73–4.

Reference in Reading

K. B. Jensen (1986) *Making Sense of the News*, Aarhus University Press.

Questions

1. What does it mean to suggest that the central role of news is 'legitimation'?
2. Why does Jensen suggest that, although viewers use TV news for a variety of purposes, ultimately they are unable to escape from its hegemonic role?
3. As an example of the 'cultural effects' school of media research, the reading asserts the power of the news in constructing and sustaining

certain social meanings. Do television programmes other than the news have the same power? Give illustrations in your answer.

Further Questions

1. Critically examine sociological explanations of the effects of the mass media on their audiences. (*AEB 1989*)
2. Examine the role of the mass media in the process of deviance amplification. (*AEB 1987*)
3. Is it useful to think of social science research as an instrument of social control? Give reasons for your answer.
4. Discuss the view that to study the effects of the media is to study the control of the powerless by the powerful.
5. Despite growing awareness of the complexity of issues involved in studying media effects, deep distrust of the media persists. Why should this be?

Further Reading

W. Belson (1978) *Television Violence and the Adolescent Boy*, Saxon House.

S. Cohen (1989) *Folk Devils and Moral Panics: the Creation of the Mods and Rockers*, Blackwell.

S. Cohen and J. Young (eds) (1973) *The Manufacture of News: Social Problems, Deviance and the Mass Media*, Constable.

L. Curtis (1986) *Ireland and the Propaganda War: The British Media and the Battle for Hearts and Minds*, Pluto Press.

J. Halloran (ed.) (1970) *The Effects of Television*, Granada.

J. Hartley (1982) *Understanding News*, Methuen.

M. Hollingsworth (1986) *The Press and Political Dissent: A Question of Censorship*, Pluto Press.

K. B. Jensen (1986) *Making Sense of The News*, Aarhus University Press.

D. McQuail, J. Blumler and J. R. Brown (1972) 'The television audience: a revised perspective', in D. McQuail (ed.) *Sociology of Mass Communications*, Penguin.

L. Masterman (1984) 'The Battle of Orgreave', in L. Masterman (ed.) *Television Mythologies*, Comedia.

P. Schlesinger, G. Murdock and P. Elliott (1983) *Televising Terrorism: Political Violence in Popular Culture*, Routledge.

6 Audience responses

How do people use the media? Do they just sit there like empty vessels being filled up with all the ideological messages that come from the media? By examining the many different uses that people put the media to we suggest a far more complex relationship between media output and audience response. Two important factors that create differing responses are: first, the social context in which the media is used; continually interrupted TV viewing is very different from the solitude of the cinema. Second, each member of the audience is a product of different social locations, hence different cultural competencies. The time and the motivation to watch are also important.

The 'uses and gratifications' approach assumes that individuals use the media to fulfil certain needs. For instance, Paul Willis (1990) argues that the use of the media, what he calls symbolic creativity, is an integral part of the human condition. An attempt to explore the relationship between uses and effects was developed by the Centre for Contemporary Cultural Studies who established the encoding/decoding analysis. They examined the process of media messages production (encoding) and then related this to media message reception and use (decoding). Reading 1 sets out the finer details of this approach.

The actual social situation that we are in, and the social relationships which inform the interactions of the people we are with when we use the media, are significant in influencing our responses. A study by Peter Collett (1985) who placed a video camera, microphone and timing device in the living room of twenty different families found a variety of different responses, ranging from total engagement to complete oblivion. He argues that people spend hours doing all kinds of things that have nothing to do with TV viewing while the set is on.

Thus, when the *Cultural Trends* (Policy Studies Institute) report notes that 98 per cent of the population watch TV on average for over 25 hours per week, it is unlikely that their attention is focused entirely on the television. As Jane Root (1986, Chapter 4, Reading 1) notes: 'people engage in an almost bizarre variety of different activities in front of the set; we eat dinner, knit jumpers, argue with each other, listen to music, read books, do our homework, kiss, write letters and vacuum clean the carpet.' So in order to understand how the media can affect us we need to ask are we open to it having any effect at all?

Both Readings 2 and 5, although focusing on very different media, *The Sun* and romantic fiction respectively, examine how the media can take on a significance in people's everyday lives. Just as Dorothy Hobson (1990) found that TV was part of the daily life of women workers, which they used as part of their general discourse on their own lives, Mark Pursehouse and Janice Radway (Readings 2 and 5) demonstrate that the media are used to structure time and communication with others. Uses of the domestic media inevitably become intertwined with household relationships: what can be seen to be the politics of the household situation.

This importance of social location is developed in Reading 3 which shows how different community members from a variety of different ethnic origins are able to negotiate the meanings of the text by confronting it with their own traditions and experience: Rambo is celebrated as an Aboriginal freedom fighter. This reading also suggests that the media provides viewers with a forum to discuss issues of concern to them.

In previous chapters we have introduced the ideas of cultural capital and habitus which suggest that the meaning that a reader constructs will depend on where they are located in relation to different discourses, knowledges and resistances. The final readings in this chapter explore the debates surrounding social difference and location. Jensen (1990) argues that the differences between particular groups is negligible in comparison to the power the media has to provide definitions of what is legitimate. Thus we need to ask: what power do readers have to make certain types of reading and does this affect their ability to challenge their subordination? For instance, Richard Dyer (1979) argues that the anarchy of capitalism throws up commodities that an oppressed group can take up and use to cobble together its own culture. Hence, gay men are able to celebrate 'Prisoner Cell Block H' by focusing on campness and on the constraints that the programme explores. Similarly, Janice Radway (Reading 5) shows how readers of romance use it to create a space from the demands of domestic pressures, Ien Ang's Dallas viewers (Reading 4) use it to create fantasies to overcome their powerlessness and Mr Cope in Valerie Walkerdine's study (Reading 6) uses Rocky to ameliorate the alienation and powerlessness that he experiences being a working-class man. However, Walkerdine (1986), urges caution with these approaches, for she maintains, whilst social locations may be important, people are not pre-determined.

A media text may provide more than one reading, i.e. it may be polysemic, which enables different individuals to construct different meanings from it. We also introduce the notion of intertextuality, that is, as Lawrence Grossberg (1987) notes: that every media event is mediated by other texts, so it is almost impossible to know what would be a pure reading of one piece of media transmission. For instance, a study by Corner, Richardson and Fenton (1990) on how people make sense of issues surrounding nuclear energy leads them to develop the concepts of 'textualization' and 're-textualization', which suggest that TV messages are reworked in people's talk as they evaluate and interpret what they see and hear.

Raymond Williams (1973) maintains that the media constructs 'structures of feelings' as the means by which the audience can engage with the media. For instance, Ien Ang (1985) in the study of Dallas in Reading 4, suggests that recognition of similar feelings to those in the programme is what most of her research respondents found pleasurable. Valerie Walkerdine (1986), however, found that the pleasure that her male respondent gained was in fact a cover for the anxiety he experienced. In a later article, Ang (1990) has argued that the pleasure that readers gain from Dallas may well be a means for dealing with powerlessness. She argues that Dallas offers a fantasy of the pleasure of imaginary identification in which the viewer is given an opportunity to take up positions which they could not do in real life; they are able momentarily to move away from the structural boundaries that constrain them.

References

I. Ang (1990) 'Melodramatic Identifications: television fiction and women's fantasy', in M. E. Brown (ed.) *Television and Women's Culture: the politics of the popular*, Sage, pp. 75–89.

I. Ang (1985) *Watching Dallas*, Methuen, pp. 5–6, 9–10, 17, 20–1, 23.

P. Collett and R. Lamb (1985) *Watching People Watching Television*, unpublished report to the Independent Broadcasting Association.

J. Corner, K. Richardson and N. Fenton (1990) 'Textualizing risk: TV discourse and the issue of nuclear energy', *Media, Culture and Society*, Vol. 12, No. 1, pp. 105–25.

R. Dyer (1979) 'In defense of disco', in S. Frith and A. Goodwin (eds) (1990) *On Record: Rock, Pop and the Written Word*, Routledge.

D. Hobson (1990) 'Women audiences and the workplace', in M. E. Brown (ed.) *Television and Women's Culture: the politics of the popular*, Sage, pp. 61–75.

K. B. Jensen (1990) 'The politics of polysemy: television news, everyday consciousness and political action', in *Media, Culture and Society*, Vol. 12, pp. 73–4.

J. Root (1986) *Open the Box: About Television*, Comedia/Channel 4.

V. Walkerdine (1986) 'Video Replay: families, films and fantasy', in V. Burgin, J. Donald, C. Kaplan (eds) *Formations of Fantasy*, Methuen, pp. 167–200.

R. Williams (1973) 'Base and superstructure in Marxist cultural theory', *New Left Review*, Vol. 82, December, pp. 3–16.

P. Willis (1990) *Common Culture: symbolic work at play in the everyday cultures of the young*, Open University Press.

☐ Encoding/Decoding

David Morley (1989), in Reading 1, sets out the premises of the encoding/decoding model which has provided the basis for a significant proportion of reader–reception theory. He argues that the important concepts of preferred readings and polysemic readings need to be used in any analysis.

Reading 1

Firstly, they [reference to the Centre for Contemporary Cultural Studies, where the theory was generated] argued that the production of a meaningful message in TV discourse is always problematic 'work'. The focus was on why certain production practices and structures tended to produce certain messages, which embody their meanings in certain recurring forms. Secondly, they argued that all messages contain more than one 'reading'. They are polysemic. They may prefer certain messages, but these can never be guaranteed. Thirdly, the activity of 'getting meaning' from a message is a problematic practice. Messages encoded in one way can always be read in different ways. In this approach, Morley argues the message is neither a unilateral sign, nor a disparate sign which can be read in any way (according to the uses and gratifications approach). The TV message is treated as a complex sign, in which a preferred reading has been inscribed, but which retains the potential, if decoded in a manner different from the way in which it has been encoded, of communicating a different meaning. The message is thus a structured polysemy. It is central to the argument that all meanings do not exist in equality, it has been structured in dominance, although its meaning can never be totally fixed or 'closed'. Further, the 'preferred reading' is itself part of the message. This model also represented an attempt to develop an analysis of the role of social structure in distributing different forms of cultural competence throughout different sections of the media audience. More recently, Morley (1989), has identified a whole number of shortcomings within this approach. For instance, the extent to which the model tends to conceive of language merely as a conveyor belt for preconstituted meanings or messages; the way in which it tends to confuse textual meaning with the conscious intention of broadcasters; and the tendency to blur together under the heading of 'decoding' what are thought of as separate processes along the axes of comprehension/incomprehension, as opposed to agreement/disagreement. The concept of preferred reading has also been subject to a number of criticisms. What for instance is the similarity between the preferred reading of a news item to that of a fictional form? There are also problems about the exact status of the 'preferred reading'. Is it something which is in the text (a property of the text) or is it something which can be generated from the text by certain methods? . . . However, I would still want to defend the model, in so far as it avoids sliding straight from the notion of a text as having a determinate meaning to an equally absurd and opposite position, in which it is assumed that the text is completely 'open' to the reader and is merely the site on which the reader constructs meaning. The point of the preferred reading model was to insist that readers, are of course, engaged in productive work, but under determinate conditions. Those determinate conditions are of course supplied both by the text, the producing institution and by the social history of the audience . . . The most useful work which has been conducted within audience studies over the last few years is that which has taken on board the questions raised about the flow of television, the positioning of the subject, the contextual determinations operating on different types of viewing of different media, alongside a close attention to patterns of taste, response and interpretation on the part of specific members of the audience.

Source

D. Morley (1989) 'Changing paradigms in audience studies', in E. Seiter, H. Borchers, G. Kreutzner and E. M. Warth (eds), *Remote Control: Television Audiences and Cultural Power*, Routledge, pp. 16–44.

Questions

1. How do we understand the relationship between the audience and the media through this approach?
2. What are the problems with the preferred reading model?
3. Why can a text never be completely open to the reader?

☐ Reading
The Sun

The Sun newspaper is often dismissed as a comic. Pursehouse (1987, Reading 2) examines the value it has in peoples' lives. By concentrating on the views of Adrian, a *Sun* reader, he demonstrates how the paper provides routine; a means of speaking to other workers and vicarious pleasure in other's worlds. This analysis is similar to Holland's (1987) work, which suggests that above other considerations, *The Sun* enables people to have a laugh.

Reference

P. Holland (1987) 'The Page Three Girl speaks to women, too', in R. Betterton (ed.), *Looking On: Images of Femininity in the Visual Arts and Media*, Pandora.

Reading 2

One 'reception site' on which *The Sun*'s discourse will be welcomed or repelled is the personal level. First, *The Sun* fits into Adrian's life in a very neat and satisfactory way. The paper has become part of the routine of his working day. It is habitually bought, and read at regular times of the day. It is a means of entertainment during work breaks and provides companionship as the entertainment role is enjoyed by fellow workers. The routine regularity of *The Sun*'s content, style and lay-out creates this comforting, reliable intersection with the regularity of the working day.

The next level of intersection or conflict is the area of personal feelings and interests. Adrian finds an identification and involvement in the paper which makes for an 'active' reading (as opposed to 'inactive' reading, at the conscious level of simply finding something to do, or the detached reading of critical analysis). When Adrian reads *The Sun* this 'involved' reading is evident in his search for sports information, his search for a laugh, a glance at what is on television, and the pleasure be obtains from the sexual presentation of females ... It is notable that when asked about what he remembers from the paper he produces a catalogue of names, not issues or incidents. The key to this personal level of intersection is that the paper is 'not serious'. *The Sun* is given credit over other papers for its efforts in satisfying the workers' search for pleasure. This pleasure is actively found in personal interests, people and titillation.

... It is by providing the satisfaction of fitting Adrian's needs that *The Sun* can form and limit Adrian's perspective. Adrian's decoding intersects with *The Sun* at the following sites of negotiation: linguistic understanding, the life-pattern, personal pleasures, and agreement with the overtly expressed and recognised representations of the world. The ideological framework of reference and its significance is not one of the negotiable areas for the reader, which is why class-conflict does not oppositionally affect Adrian's creation of meaning.

... Adrian does not ask himself about class and power when reading. He asks, 'do I understand?'; 'does it fit in my life-style?'; 'do I feel any pleasure?' and; 'do I mainly agree with its view-point?' Adrian is satisfied by *The Sun*'s answer to these questions ... There is no female equivalent for the companionship the paper provides for the men on the building site. *The Sun* does not enter or even recognise the female working world ... whilst the pleasure of the male gazing at the female body is a major 'use' of the paper ...

Whatever the variety these interviews present they have in common features which reveal the success of *The Sun*. Each person finds some surface level 'uses' for *The Sun* and while page three may be a big draw for men, women can ignore its offensive treatment if it is overshadowed by some other personal pleasure. The text is negotiated along the question of whether individual items relate to personal interests and experiences ... It is read as a routine, regular habit and joins the routine, regular nature of daily life, as a companion in the closed, personal world ... It is not read without criticism. Nobody is impressed with its record for accuracy and the 'scandal' element is not as welcome as the keener interest in more than honest, human stories, which *The Sun* does not adequately cover. These features can also detract from *The Sun* persona ... There is a similar criticism of the overworked 'corny' phraseology ... It is also interesting that the excess of royalty coverage gets heavily criticised ... There is virtually a unanimous denial that the paper has any notable 'meaning' to them beyond the personal 'uses'.

Source

M. Pursehouse (1987) 'Life's more fun with your number one Sun': Interviews with some Sun readers, Stencilled Occasional Paper, No. 85. Birmingham, Centre for Contemporary Cultural Studies.

Questions

1. What functions does *The Sun* fill in Adrian's life? Why?
2. How does *The Sun* intersect with Adrian's social location and cultural capital?
3. How does *The Sun* limit and contain the questions that Adrian can ask about inequalities, such as the class structure, racism and sexism?

□ Reading Rambo

From research which examined international readings of Dallas, Katz and Leibes (1986) found different community members from a variety of different ethnic origins negotiated the meaning of Dallas by confronting it with their own traditions and experience.

Reference

T. Leibes and E. Katz (1986) 'Patterns of involvement in television fiction: a comparative analysis', *European Journal of Communication*, Vol. 1, No. 2, pp. 151–71.

Reading 3

Michaels (1986) found that *Rambo* was one of the most popular movies among Aborigines living a tribal life in the deserts of central Australia. They made their meanings out of the text, for they understood the major conflict to be that between *Rambo*, whom they saw as a representative of the third world, and the white officer class – a set of meanings that were clearly relevant to their experience of white, post-colonial paternalism and that may well have been functional in helping them to make a resistant sense of their interracial relationships. The Aborigines also produced tribal or kinship relations between *Rambo* and the prisoner he was rescuing that were more relevant to their social experience than any national-istic relationships structured around the East–West axis. Aborigines do, after all, occupy a massively disproportionate number of places in Australian prisons.

Source

J. Fiske (1989) *Understanding Popular Culture*, Unwin Hyman, p. 57.

References in Reading

E. Michaels (1986) *Aboriginal Content*, Paper presented to the meeting of the Australian Screen Studies Association, Sydney.

Questions

1. How were the Aborigines able to use *Rambo* to make sense of their own experiences? What does this suggest about the relationship between the media and the audience?
2. In Reading 1, David Morley suggests that media programmes offer the audience a preferred reading. What is the preferred reading of *Rambo* likely to be and how do the Aborigines challenge it?
3. Is it possible to see *Rambo* as a racist text when Aborigines are able to subvert the meanings for themselves? Give reasons for your answer.

☐ Emotional Realism

According to Adorno and Horkheimer (1977) the experience of pleasure in mass culture is a false kind of pleasure, even part of the trick of manipulating the masses more effectively in order to lock them in the external status quo of exploitation and oppression. Ang (1985) suggests in the following reading that it may be more complex.

Reference

T. Adorno and M. Horkheimer (1977) 'The culture industry', in J. Curran, M. Gurevitch and J. Woollacott (eds), *Mass Communication and Society*, Edward Arnold/Open University.

Reading 4

In order to obtain information on the way in which people experience watching *Dallas*, I placed a small advertisement in a Dutch women's magazine called *Viva*, which read as follows:

> I like watching the TV serial *Dallas*, but often get odd reactions to it. Would anyone like to write and tell me why you like watching it too, or dislike it? I should like to assimilate these reactions in my university thesis. Please write to . . .

I had forty-two replies to this advertisement. Letters, all addressed personally to me, varying in length from a few lines to around ten pages. All the letters except three were written by individuals. One letter was written by two boys and two girls, two letters by two girls. Only one letter was anonymous, all the others were provided with the sender's name and in most cases the address too. From these names it emerges that only three letters were from boys or men. The rest were written by girls or women.

Why do people watch *Dallas*? Clearly because they find it enjoyable. Nobody is forced to watch television; at most, people can be led to it by effective advertising. What then are the determining factors of this enjoyment, this pleasure? Sociologists often start with the premise that media use is determined by people's needs and the gratifications they expect. However, the attention given to the socio-psychological constitution of (individual) viewers implies a functionalist conception of pleasure in which its essence is regarded as the experience of satisfaction whenever a certain pre-existent need is fulfilled. What is completely ignored in this conception are the *mechanisms* by which pleasure is aroused. What are the characteristics of *Dallas* that organize the viewer's pleasure? This question indicates that pleasure must be conceived of as not so much the automatic result of some satisfaction of needs, but rather as the effect of a certain productivity of a cultural artefact. Evidently,

Dallas offers entertainment, but what is it about *Dallas* that makes it a favourite item of entertainment, and what precisely does its entertainment value consist of? . . . but we should rather ask ourselves what happens in the process of watching *Dallas*. Is it in the actual confrontation between viewer and programme that pleasure is primarily generated?

Pleasure is equated with entertainment; in which fun is not only presented as perfectly legitimate but also as being in opposition to 'boring information or education' . . . I want to concentrate my attention on a phenomenon, one aspect of popularity which is in itself complex enough: pleasure.

Popular pleasure is first and foremost a pleasure of recognition . . . Pleasure in *Dallas* is therefore associated with the pleasure of the freedoms of entertainment, in which people feel released from the prohibitions and demands of society . . . However we cannot take the pleasure of *Dallas* on its own terms. This has to do with the authoritarian character of television programming: it is the television networks which decide which programmes are to be broadcast and which not. The audience can only wait and see what menu it will be served. In this sense the television audience is passive. It could then be reasoned that people watch *Dallas* for the lack of anything better.

Source

I. Ang (1985) *Watching Dallas*, Methuen, pp. 5–6, 9–10, 17, 20–1, 23.

Questions

1. Is the pleasure that Ien Ang's respondents mentioned a false pleasure as Adorno and Horkheimer would suggest?
2. If a television programme is pleasurable, does this necessarily mean that it stops people being critical of it?
3. Ang suggests that it is the mechanisms of pleasure that are important. What modes of pleasure do you think *Dallas* uses?

□ Romance as Independence?

Drawing upon Hobson's (1982) work which uses empirical research to investigate how women's domestic situation structures their relationship to the media and which finds that housewives use the media to counter the isolation which they experience, Radway (1987, below) finds from her study of a group of women in Smithton that they use romantic fiction to preserve a private world of pleasurable fantasy within the pressures of their domestic role.

Reference

D. Hobson (1982) *Crossroads: the Drama of a Soap Opera*, Methuen.

Reading 5

Reading the Romance turns to Fish's notion of 'interpretive communities' to theorise regularities and then attempts to determine whether the Smithton women operate on romances as an interpretive community . . . it was the women readers' construction of the act of romance reading as a 'declaration of independence' that surprised me into the realization that the meaning of their media-use was multiply determined and internally contradictory and that to get at its complexity it would be helpful to distinguish analytically between the significance of the *event* of reading and meaning of the *text* constructed as its consequence. Although I did not then formulate it in so many words, this notion of the event of reading directed me towards a series of questions about the uses 'to which a particular text is put, its function within a particular conjuncture, in particular institutional spaces, and in relation to particular audiences'. What the book gradually became, then, was less an account of the way romances as texts were interpreted than of the way romance reading as a form of behaviour operated as a complex intervention in the ongoing social life of actual social subjects, women who saw themselves first as wives and mothers.

As a consequence, *Reading the Romance* bears striking similarities to Dorothy Hobson's *Crossroads* (1982), to the work on the TV programme *Nationwide* by David Morley and Charlotte Brunsdson (1978), and to Angela McRobbie's (1978) work on the culture of working-class girls. Although the central problematic of the book is not formulated in the languages they employ, nor is their work cited specifically, *Reading the Romance* shares their preoccupation with questions about the degree of freedom audiences demonstrate in their interaction with media messages and their interest in the way such cultural forms are embedded in the social life of their users. The theoretical position taken up in the book is quite close to Dorothy Hobson's conclusion that 'there is no overall intrinsic message or meaning in the work', and that 'it comes alive and communicates when the viewers add their own interpretation and understanding to the programme'. Indeed, because I agreed at the outset with Stanley Fish's claim that textual features are not an essential structure upon which an interpretation is hung but rather produced *through* the interpretive process, I think the theoretical position of *Reading the Romance* is also close to Hobson's additional observation that 'there can be as many interpretations of a programme (or text) as the individual viewers bring to it'. However, the book argues additionally that whatever the theoretical possibility of an infinite number of readings, in fact, there are patterns or regularities to what viewers and readers bring to texts and media messages in large part because they acquire specific cultural competencies as a consequence of their particular social location.

Source

J. Radway (1987) *Reading the Romance*, University of North Carolina Press, pp. 5, 7–8.

References in Reading

C. Brunsdon and D. Morley (1978) *Everyday Television: 'Nationwide'*, British Film Institute.

A. McRobbie (1978) *'Jackie': an Ideology of Adolescent Femininity*, Centre for Contemporary Cultural Studies, Stencilled Paper No. 53, University of Birmingham.

Questions

1. Why is the Smithton women's use of romance multiple determined and internally contradictory?
2. Why is it useful to distinguish between the significance of the reading event and the meaning of the text?
3. Why is this account of what people do with the media significantly different from all previous accounts?

□ Overcoming Powerlessness

Television viewing not only fits into the domestic routines and practices of a family, it is also influenced by the gendered and class power relationships of the household. By focusing on how a family watch *Rocky*, Walkerdine (1986) is also able to show how fantasies become inscribed within the domestic situation.

Reading 6

I try to show how aspects of the filmic representations are incorporated into the domestic practices of the family. There is, in this watching, a moment of *creation* – if it is effective and successful as a cultural product for the mass market whose desires it helps to form. There is certainly an aesthetic or a pleasure. An aesthetic is cold. What I am talking about is red hot. It is what makes the youths in cinema audiences cheer and scream for Rocky to win the match – including many black youths, even though the Mr Big of boxing, whom he defeats, is black. It is what makes Mr Cole [the father of the family] want to have the fight on continuous and instant replay forever, to live in the triumph of that moment. And it is what makes me throb with pain. Although it is easy to dismiss such films as macho, stupid, fascist, it is more revealing to see them as fantasies of omnipotence, heroism and salvation. They can thus be understood as a counterpoint to the experience of oppression and powerlessness. Fighting in the film, is related to a class-specific and gendered use of the body. Rocky's body is constantly presented as beaten, mutilated and punished. The film always presents this body as spectacle and triumph, triumph over and through that mutilation, which is the desperate fear that fuels it. The fantasy of the fighter is the fantasy of a working-class male omnipotence over the forces of humiliating oppression which mutilate and break the body in *manual* labour. Power in its manifest content covers over a terror of powerlessness, an anxiety beneath the pleasure. Mr Cole is afraid of being 'soft', of a femininity lurking beneath the surface . . . Identifications, like those of Rocky and Mr Cole as fighters, may be fictions inscribed in fantasy, set and worked out in the film itself, but they are also lived out in practices in which Mr Cole is inserted. There is no 'real' of these practices which stands outside fantasy, no split between fantasy as a psychic space and a reality which can be known. If such fictional identities become 'real' in practice, they must have a psychical reality which has a positive effectivity in the lived materiality of the practices of themselves. Such fictional identities must be created in the plays of power and desire. They are also therefore created in relational dynamics in which others can project fantasies on to, and invest them in, subjects within the family and other relations . . . We need to understand how these 'lived relations' are formed through regimes of meanings which position the participants and which 'lock into' relations of signification in the media ... Reading and viewing can be a place of desperate dreaming, of hope for transformation (pp. 168–89).

Source

V. Walkerdine (1986) 'Video Replay: families, films and fantasy', in V. Burgin, J. Donald and C. Kaplan (eds) *Formations of Fantasy*, Methuen, pp. 167–200.

Questions

1. What dimensions does this reading add to our understanding of how audiences use the media, and how the status quo is reproduced in this process?
2. How are aspects of filmic representation incorporated into the domestic practices of the family?
3. Walkerdine reveals pleasure to be a cover for anxiety, are women watching Rocky likely to respond in a similar way? Give reasons for your answer.

General Questions

1. From the readings in this chapter what are the main uses that people put the media to, and why do they use the media in these ways?
2. Is it possible to understand how people use the media without understanding both their social location and the context in which the media is being received? Give reasons for your answer.
3. The final three extracts suggest that people's use of the media is a coping strategy for overcoming powerlessness and alienation. How can this be seen to be part of the processes of incorporation and control?
4. Does this chapter suggest that people are empty vessels having their heads filled up with whatever media messages come their way? Use the readings to provide evidence for your answer.

Further Reading

I. Ang (1985) *Watching Dallas: Soap Opera and the Melodramatic Imagination*, Methuen.

C. Brunsdon and D. Morley (1978) *Television Monograph. Everyday Television: 'Nationwide'*, British Film Institute.

P. Holland (1987) 'The Page Three Girl speaks to women too.' In R. Betterton (ed.) *Looking On: Images of Femininity in the Visual Arts and Media*, Pandora, pp. 93–105.

T. Modleski (1982) *Loving with Vengeance: mass-produced fantasies for women*, Shoe String Press.

D. Morley (1986) *Family Television. Cultural Power and Domestic Leisure,* Comedia.

J. Root (1986) *Open the Box: About Television,* Comedia.

E. Seiter, H. Borchers, G. Kreutzner and E. M. Warth (1989) *Remote Control: Television, Audiences and Cultural Power*, Routledge.

7 | New technology

The 1990s and beyond will see the media assume ever greater social, economic and cultural significance. Appropriately, in this final chapter, we consider the current debates that surround the present and future development of the media. The advent of so-called 'new technology', particularly in broadcasting, has led to national and international debate about the future of radio and television: how much of it ought there to be; in what ways should it be made available to the viewing and listening public; who should make programmes and how should they be financed; what type of programmes should we expect; how much control will traditional regulatory bodies established by the state be able to exercise; who will own the 'new' media?

In spite of the fact that the mass media as we experience them in the late twentieth century would not have developed without the utilisation of specific technologies, it is not unusual for any discussion of the media's purpose or effectivity to ignore the importance of these technological determinants. It is as if the technology were somehow 'just there', natural but invisible. This final chapter challenges this assumption for two main reasons.

Firstly, we would argue that it is naive to assume that technology and technological determinants are in some way neutral, detached and distanced from those issues of power and control which have been the focus for discussion throughout this book. Rather, it seems important to raise questions about the relationship between technology and its social use, to acknowledge that technological development depends upon the social relations of its inception.

Second, and in spite of the comments above, contemporary debate about media policy, both within a national and international context, seems driven by the apparent obligation to utilise the so-called 'new technology', particularly satellite and cable. Often, discussion about broadcasting policy, the future shape and structure of radio and television, seems to start from the point of view that the new technologies must inevitably dictate policy whatever other factors are involved.

In many respects, this foregrounding of technology is to be welcomed if we are to understand developments in today's media.

Whether discussing broadcasting policy, or a specific aesthetic form such as music video, technological determinants are clearly an influential factor. In the print media the application of new technology enabling journalists to make direct inputs using computers has made a radical difference, leading to a massive restructuring of the industry and consequent unemployment for traditional print workers. In trying to understand these developments, we need to consider the relationship between technological and other determinants – political, economic, ideological, regulatory – which are also operative.

☐ The Implications of the New Technology in Broadcasting

Some commentators would argue that the pace and scale of technological change is such that it seems to be sweeping aside all other considerations. This is particularly the case in broadcasting, where transnational developments in cable and satellite seem to be challenging the relevance of national media policies.

Reading 1

The last decade has seen an enormous change in the television broadcasting scene across the world. Cable systems and satellite broadcasting – and particularly the marriage of these two technologies – have brought about a phenomenal increase in the available channels of television entertainment and video communication. Broadcasting by satellite has enabled the subscriber to a cable system, whether in the USA or Britain or Sweden, to gain access to a wide range of material previously undreamt of. But these two technologies have other implications which are usually less visible: both technologies are important culturally and industrially. For these reasons, it is necessary to consider them not only within the context of more broadcasting entertainment but also within the context of national states planning for their future industrial needs and cultural desires. And, because the various forms of broadcasting by satellite straddle national frontiers, there are implications for those nations who desire to retain and encourage their own cultures in the face of foreign broadcasting . . .

Each nation state will experience these changes in a different way and, even more importantly, not all nations will perceive the new media as a threat to their industrial development and to their existing structures of broadcasting. Many are likely to welcome the additional channels of entertainment, the diversity in telecommunications delivery and the new era of broadcasting competition. Similarly, it is possible that whilst policy makers and public service broadcasters may fear the impact of the new media, the viewing public will look to them for an escape from the limited fare on offer . . .

There is some sort of unity of concern across Europe, for example, where public service organizations under some form of state control have until the recent past been dominant. These organizations are soon to face immense competition from an array of eager entrepreneurs as their monopolistic position is rapidly eroded.

[In the] next decade – and assuming that all current plans for new television services come to fruition – television broadcasting across Europe will have been transformed . . . Cable systems will exist side by side with 'low', 'medium' and 'high' power satellite systems as well as traditional forms of terrestrial broadcasting systems. Each of these systems will attempt to offer something unique and the viewer will face the unenviable task of exercising a very difficult choice . . . the changes will range across hardware and software; they will impact on existing broadcasting structures, on sources of funding, on programme producers, on regulators and on many other groups and institutions which are connected . . . with 'the media', both old and new . . .

Whether these additional services enrich the menu rather than simply increase its length is . . . an issue of little consequence. The changes currently taking place are at such an advanced stage of development that academic or even policy debates matter little in the rapidly changing world of the new media. The speed of technological change and the inability (or unwillingness) of governments across the world to plan the direction of these developments, has given them the look of an unstoppable force. In some European countries there has been an acquiescence on the part of the regulatory and governmental agencies – acquiescence since it is typified by an unwillingness to debate the wider issues of the place of the broadcast media in the cultural, social and political life of a nation state – which has allowed the technological rollercoaster to move unobstructed by political or social concerns.

Source

Ralph Negrine (ed.) (1988) *Satellite Broadcasting: The Politics and Implications of the New Media*, Routledge, pp. 1–3.

Questions

1. Why are the new technologies of cable and satellite important both culturally and industrially?
2. In what ways does the new broadcasting technology challenge national broadcasting policies?
3. Why might some European countries have acquiesced in the speed and scope of technological change?

☐ New Technology and Broadcasting in the UK

That there is a relationship between technological and other determinants was acknowledged in the 1988 White Paper on broadcasting, the blueprint for the recent Broadcasting Act. Arguing that 'because of technological, international and other developments, change is inevitable', the White Paper outlined a set of proposals for the future of both radio and television in the UK.

Reading 2

There are bound to be uncertainties about the nature and pace of change. Even so there are a number of developments already in train which, even if Government were to take no action, would affect the broadcasting environment.

– Broadcasting and telecommunications are increasingly converging. Technological developments are making possible, and very probably economic, the delivery of additional services in new ways. By one means or another the limitations imposed by spectrum scarcity are likely to be overcome or bypassed.
– This means that more programmes will be feasible, both domestically and internationally. Some of these will develop whatever the attitude of the Government.
– Technology will make possible the provision of improved sound

and visual images. A new high quality transmission standard, MAC (Multiplexed Analogue Components), is being introduced for DBS (direct broadcasting by satellite) services. There is also the prospect of satellite-delivered high definition television services, using the MAC-compatible system being developed by a consortium of European industry and broadcasters.

– Direct payment for television programme services is likely to grow significantly. The development of the market for video rental and for prerecorded video tapes is evidence of the demand, and technology for subscription, including pay per view, now exists . . .

– as delivery systems proliferate, national frontiers begin to blur or disappear. There will be increasing demand from an international market for programme material. Programme services of international reach are likely to develop further. There will be increasing interest in the scope for agreement on programme standards, particularly within Europe.

– With increasing prosperity, and greater leisure time and expenditure, the audio-visual sector is likely to become more important in advanced economies.

Source

Home Office (1988) *Broadcasting in the '90s: Competition, Choice and Quality*, White Paper on Broadcasting, HMSO, pp. 4–5.

Questions

1. What are the new technologies identified in the White Paper, and what is the underlying attitude towards technological determinism?
2. What other determinants does the White Paper introduce as being of importance?
3. In what ways, and why, does the White Paper make a number of questionable assumptions?

☐ Technology and its Social Use

Contemporary broadcasting policy in the UK has been dominated by the drive to establish regulatory structures based on market forces, in the belief that these will deliver a wider viewer and listener choice. What has often been called a policy of deregulation is in fact a policy of re-regulation, establishing a specific set of broadcasting structures which challenge existing concepts of public service broadcasting and legitimise making programmes for profit. Such structures are determined by political, economic and ideological considerations as much by technological imperatives. For example, given that cable television has been available since the 1950s, it seems reasonable to ask why its utilisation is suddenly so necessary. Williams offers a more complex model of the relationship between technology and its social use.

Reading 3

We have now become used to a situation in which broadcasting is a major social institution, about which there is always controversy but which, in its familiar form, seems to have been predestined by the technology. This predestination however, when closely examined, proves to be no more than a set of particular social decisions, in particular circumstances, which were then so widely if imperfectly ratified that it is now difficult to see them as decisions rather than as (retrospectively) inevitable results.

Thus, if seen only in hindsight, broadcasting can be diagnosed as a new and powerful form of social integration and control. Many of its main uses can be seen as socially, commercially and at times politically manipulative. Moreover, this viewpoint is rationalized by its description as 'mass communication', a phrase used by all its agents and advisers as well, curiously, as by most of its radical critics. 'Masses' had been the new nineteenth-century term of contempt for what was formerly described as 'the mob' . . . A new radical class-consciousness adopted the term to express the material of new social formations: 'mass organizations'. The 'mass meeting' was an observable physical effect . . . mass now meant large numbers rather than any physical or social aggregate. Sound radio and television, for reasons we shall look at, were developed for transmission to *individual* homes, though there was nothing in the technology to make this inevitable. But then this new form of social communication – broadcasting – was obscured by its definition as 'mass communication'; an abstraction to its most general characteristic, that it went to many people, 'the masses', which obscured the fact that the means chosen was the offer of individual sets, a method much better described by the earlier word 'broadcasting'. It is interesting that the only developed 'mass' use of radio was in Nazi Germany, where under Goebbels' orders the Party organized compulsory public listening groups and the receivers were in the streets . . .

State intervention in broadcasting had some real and some plausible technical grounds: the distribution of wavelengths. But to these were added, though always controversially, more general social directions or attempts at direction. This social history of broadcasting can be discussed on its own . . . [but] it is unrealistic to extract it from another and more decisive process, through which, in particular economic situations, a set of scattered technical devices become an applied technology and then a social technology . . .

In capitalist democracies, the thrust for conversion from scattered techniques to a technology was not political but economic. The characteristically isolated inventors, from Nipkow and Rosing to Baird and Jenkins and Zwyorkin, found their point of development, if at all, in the manufacturers and prospective manufacturers of the technical apparatus. The history at one level is that of these isolated names, but at another level it is of EMI, RCA and a score of similar companies and corporations . . . In broadcasting, both in sound radio and later in television, the major investment was in the means of distribution, and was devoted to production only so far as to make the distribution technically possible and then attractive . . . It is not only that the supply of broadcasting facilities preceded the demand; it is that the means of communication preceded their content.

Source

Raymond Williams (1974) *Television: Technology and Cultural Form*, Fontana, pp. 23–5.

Questions

1. Why is it naive to assume that broadcasting as we know it today was 'predestined' by its technology?
2. Why does Williams argue that the social history of broadcasting is about isolated names *and* companies and corporations?
3. What relevance does the extract have for the contemporary deployment of 'new technology' such as satellite and cable TV?

☐ Technological Change and Patterns of Employment

This more complex model which insists that we relate the development and utilisation of technology to its wider context informs the next extract. It is often argued that one of the 'advantages' of new technology is that it is labour-saving, as in the print industry. Within the American broadcasting industry 'network station managers are desperately seeking new technology and schemes to cut back on ever more technicians' (*Broadcast*, 15 April, 1988, p. 15), and the same process is under way in the UK. Colin Sparks relates the introduction of new technology and its effects on employment to a wider economic and political context.

Reading 4

Behind these struggles are longer-term forces, which are of two kinds: technical and politico-economic. Most of the attention to technical factors in the last few years has been concentrated upon the changing technologies of distribution, particularly upon the ability of cable and satellite transmission to both segment the TV audience and to decouple it from its traditional close correspondence with the boundaries of the nation state ... [These] allow, in principle, the transmission of the same programme to an ever-larger audience as well as the much more often noted possibility of increasing the number of available programmes. Thus they contain the potential of shifting the balance of TV production from 'variable' (wages) to 'fixed' (plant) capital and, with it, the possibility of more intense exploitation of the labour force. At the same time, they require a much larger initial investment in the means of distribution than hitherto, which must also be entirely in place before any form of broadcasting can occur.

The second, and less remarked upon, development concerns the changes taking place in the technology of production. Some of these are 'indeterminate' with regard to the rate of exploitation: the replacement of film by electronic cameras, or of film by video in the editing suite, do not in themselves mean either a change in the size of the labour force or its membership. The large-size crews operating with conventional film equipment which have been prominent features of British TV production were not necessitated by the nature of that equipment: there is, after all, a school of documentary film-making, exemplified by the work of Roger Graef, which has always produced highly regarded results with very much smaller crews than the norm. The large crews used in most TV production were thus primarily the result of union strength in collective bargaining, using technical issues as one of their counters, rather than the necessary consequence of the technology. But the fact that modern electronic cameras are lighter than previous models and that they can combine picture and sound recording in one unit, or that the function of the camera-loader is rendered obsolete by the shift from film to electronic recording, does not in itself dictate the need for fewer technicians. These developments may make it harder for the unions to produce technical arguments to support their negotiating position, but in the end the level of staffing will be determined by the relative strengths of the bargaining parties.

The introduction of electronic recording devices into, say, television drama, provides the possibility of reduced costs, but these need not necessarily arise from reduced staffing levels. The same applies to the use of electronic editing, which involves a change in technical process which can be relearned relatively easily by a film editor. However, the shift towards electronic technology and the ever-increasing use of computing in the production of TV programmes does contain within itself the drive to replace human beings with machines. The clearest example so far is the introduction of remote-controlled cameras in the studios, which has progressed some way in news and current affairs in the US:

> The de-manning of US TV is well under way. With a studio camera-man earning $80,000 a year, NBC means to make considerable man-power savings on the new [remote-controlled] cameras. CBS recently sacked 210 staff in order to cut $30 from its $300 million budget . . .

This represents a new and different kind of development which corresponds much more exactly to the normal processes of capitalist production in which the introduction of new machinery is designed explicitly to reduce labour inputs in order to secure competitive advantages.

Source

Colin Sparks (1989) 'The Impact of Technological and Political Change on the Labour Force in British Television', *Screen*, Vol. 30, Nos 1 & 2, Winter/Spring, pp. 26–7.

Questions

1. In what ways does the changing technology of broadcasting distribution enhance the power of large transnational corporations?
2. Why might it be argued that the relationship between new technology and employment is essentially about issues of power?
3. Is the writer justified in relating issues here not to 'technological predestination', but to wider issues of capitalist production?

☐ The Effects of Deregulation on Italian TV

Political decisions as to how the new technology is used affect not just the organisational structure of the broadcasting industry, but programmes as well. In particular, reliance upon advertising as a source of income has meant that, across Europe, there has been an increase in the number of broadcasting hours, as well as the amount of airtime devoted to advertising. This can be seen in the case of Italy, the first country to deregulate its broadcasting structure, so that the state system (RAI – Radiotelevisione Italiana) was faced with intense commercial competition, chiefly from Silvio Berlusconi's Fininvest group with its three channels, as well as other commercial stations. The main effects have been a lengthening of the broadcasting day, and a greater reliance on imported programmes, especially made-for-TV movies.

Reading 5

The increase in the number of broadcasting hours has been spectacular. RAI broadcast a total of 5950 programme hours in 1976. This tose to 6820 by 1978, to 9225 in 1980 and 12,225 in 1983. Then in 1986, RAI broadcast 14,500 hours and the Fininvest group 19,500, figures which rose further in 1987 to 15,900 and 19,650 respectively.

Within ten years, therefore, the supply of programmes has risen from about 6000 hours to over 34,000 ... Not only has this consumption of television by the Italian public grown enormously, but there has been a parallel increase in the amount of advertising. In 1983 the three RAI channels between them carried a total of 40,000 advertising slots. In 1987 there were over 60,000, while the three Fininvest channels carried no fewer than 284,000 in the course of the year.

This enormous increase in the amount of advertising, particularly on the private channels, led to considerable public outcry and demands in Parliament ... for a ceiling on advertising and in particular a limit on the frequency of advertising breaks in programmes such as films ...

The change from a monopoly to a mixed television system in Italy has led to an over-abundance of television programming, interspersed with regular advertising messages, and a television day covering all the waking hours ...

A second consequence of the mixed system, it has been claimed, has been a concentration of broadcasting time around particular genres at the expense of others ...

Genre	RAI		Fininvest	
	minutes	%	minutes	%
Classical music	2,233	3.3	–	–
Theatre	1,040	1.6	–	–
TV series	4,031	6.0	5,242	5.9
Films	8,317	12.4	13,967	15.6
Made-for-TV movies	3,292	4.9	34,096	38.1
Cartoons	1,429	2.1	6,971	7.8
Entertainment and quiz programmes	9,584	14.3	8,853	9.9
Light music	1,857	2.8	2,225	2.5
Documentaries	1,286	1.9	379	0.4
Reports	6,768	10.1	1,814	2.0
Education	3,374	5.1	–	–
News	7,065	10.6	–	–
News specials	1,065	1.6	649	0.7
Sport	9,945	14.9	3,060	3.4
Parliament, political discussion, open acces	541	0.8	168	0.2
Presentation and trailers	96	0.1	311	0.3
Programme publicity	703	1.1	1,909	2.1
Advertising	2,320	3.5	9,417	10.5
Other	1,908	2.9	512	0.6
Totals	66,854	100	89,573	100

The third consequence of the fierce competition between public television and the private networks lies in the way that programming strategies have become competitive not just in the fiction field ... but across the entire schedule. Take the example of news and current affairs, ... the number of news bulletins on RAI has risen from 2 per day to nearly 25 today ... The fact that the private networks are not allowed to broadcast live programmes and cannot therefore compete on level terms with RAI in areas such as news has given RAI the opportunity to make a feature of regular news bulletins as part of its schedules . . .

In a competitive regime the use of news has acquired a new strategic function, very different from that which it enjoyed in the monopoly period when it mainly served the political function of legitimising the role of the political elites. In the current situation, news programmes have been subjected to a strategy of corporate image-making, as can be seen by the way the product 'news programmes' has undergone changes of format, making it more a market-orientated genre. As the number of bulletins multiplies, and as their internal structure changes (notably with the introduction of thematic items aimed at particular sections of the market), the impact of competitive strategies becomes more and more blatant . . . Competition not only affects all parts of the schedule, but accentuates the shift from broadcasting to narrowcasting, even within television systems which in other respects remain 'generalist' in orientation.

Source

Mauro Wolf (1989 'Italy from Deregulation to a New Equilibrium', in G. Nowell-Smith (ed.) *The Broadcasting Debate: The European Experience*, British Film Institute, pp. 53–7.

Questions

1. What have been the main effects of the competitive regime in Italian television?
2. It is often claimed that the new broadcasting regimes will deliver greater choice for viewers. What conclusions can be drawn from the Italian experience?
3. Why is 'narrowcasting' a consequence of a market-orientated television service?

□ The Future for Children's Programming

Although proponents of broadcasting deregulation argue for the superiority of the market as a mechanism for gauging and reflecting audience needs, others seem concerned that future programming might ignore the needs of those whose political and economic power is limited or non-existent. Reflecting widespread concern amongst broadcasters, a Programme Controller at Tyne Tees Television voices her fears for the future of children's programmes in any new market-orientated broadcasting environment, where innovative programmes for younger viewers may be forced out because of high costs.

Reading 6

The Broadcasting White Paper makes no provision for the protection of any sort of children's programmes. BSB [British Satellite Broadcasting – merged with Sky in 1991 to form BSkyB] has abandoned plans for a children's channel and even the Royal Television Society has dropped its children's award. Channel 4 . . . barely a year after axing its children's programmes and its children's commissioning editor, is now scheduling animation, repeats and imported drama and cartoons. At the moment, however, they won't take on 'the huge expense' of commissioning new children's material.

ITV is concerned at the cost of this sort of programming and is warning that it doesn't earn its keep from the advertisers . . .

Given the financial pressure on all companies, it's easy to sympathize with this view, and children's programming will have to take its share of the financial impact . . . But the network children's sub-group is already implementing a policy of not re-commissioning programmes which don't perform well in the ratings and not commissioning at all those that don't seem to be value for money.

. . . the danger signs are there, with the temptation to schedule wall-to-wall imported cartoons or to commission co-productions, which can result in innocuous blandness, because they are cheap. 'How much will it cost?' is now a prime consideration in the commissioning of new children's material and, despite efforts to save money for new projects by the judicious use of repeats, there's not much hope for the survival of a mixed schedule which contains information, documentary or any programme that might need a second series to hit its stride.

So ITV needs the money now allocated to children's programmes but the kids prefer to watch *Neighbours*. The easy solution is to give them what they apparently want. But is that all that they want? Certainly soaps and cartoons are popular and there's nothing wrong with that, but children are sophisticated and discriminating viewers. They have easy access to feature films and videos and will quickly spot cheaply made programmes with poor production values.

They will eventually tire of cheap imports, product-led programmes and cartoons – and remember, so far we've been seeing the best of these; there's an awful lot of rubbish waiting to come in. The trouble is that children often don't want to admit to watching children's programmes and this is a serious problem in measuring the audience. Another difficulty is that this audience is not a homogeneous entity. Programmes that appeal to a four-year-old are unlikely to appeal to a 14-year-old . . .

Children's programmes have a real value but, like other areas of public service broadcasting, they are under threat . . . children have no political voice, no significant disposable income and, while more family shows might emerge, the future doesn't look rosy for special programming.

Source

Trish Kinane (1989) 'The children's hour of need approaches', *Broadcast*, 14 April 1989, p. 23.

Questions

1. Is there a case for arguing that, left to the dictates of the market, specialist programming is likely to diminish or disappear?
2. The writer makes a number of value judgements throughout the article. Is it possible to define quality with reference to television programmes?
3. What conditions might ensure that the new technology was used to provide programmes for all social sectors and interests?

□ The Neglected Audience

In this final extract, we are taken back to those concerns with which we began this book, not least the question of who controls the media and in whose interests. Few would disagree that the new technology offers exciting and challenging prospects both for the media and the related world of telecommunications. How that technology is used, by whom, and for what purpose, are issues which are being decided, not by some technological inevitability, but by political, economic and ideological considerations. Tana Wollen and Janet Willis argue that these decisions are not being made in the best interests of the audiences for broadcasting, and that this will have far-reaching consequences.

Reading 7

At the heart of the current proposals to deregulate broadcasting in Britain lies a rhetoric about the individual's freedom to choose. 'The Government's aim is to open the door so that individuals can choose for themselves from a much wider range of programmes and types of broadcasting' (1988 White Paper). Since the availability of television programmes will depend, to an increasing extent, on people's ability to pay for them, the airwaves, like gas, water and electricity, can no longer be considered as shared and regulated public resources.

These are not free choices. The range of services now available may be so destabilised as to make audiences bound to buy in to new systems. New aerials, dishes, decoders and subscriptions will make the present licence fee seem cheap at double the price. The increasing cost of advertising goods and services must also, in the end, be met by their consumers. Broadcasting will cost audiences more. The disappearance of a single, standardized fee means that information, education and entertainment will pass into more privatised realms of ownership and consumption. Television's contributions to a public culture will be divided between the information-rich and the information-poor. The wider choices are only available to those who can afford them.

As Eastern Europe opens its doors and considers the attractions of Western democracies, British television talks breathlessly of choice, the freedom to speak, the right to know. We would do well to examine the mechanisms of our own democratic processes, for the deregulation of broadcasting means that some of these are at stake. Democracy depends on information and debate being made widely available. The present duopoly [BBC and ITV] is by no means perfect in this respect but to differentiate access to public information according to the capacity of citizens to pay for it will mean their correspondingly differentiated capacity to participate within a social democracy . . .

From some perspectives the viewer and the listener, as consumers of a wider range of channels, are indeed central to this government's broadcasting policy. Whatever their technological potential, the new delivery systems will be redundant unless viewers are prepared to pay for them. No wonder that the freedom to choose not to become a consumer is not being made to appear attractive. Unless television companies can deliver viewers to the advertisers who are to sustain their broadcasting, then they will not survive the rigours of an extremely competitive climate. Customising their channels to more particular tastes and interests, television companies will have to attend to ever more fragmented clusters of viewers. It is a more particularised notion of viewers, as a collection of individuals, which is emphasised in the proposals for change. It is the notion of an audience, as people holding something in common for the length of a programme or an evening's schedule, which is being neglected.

. . . it is hard to see how the market will be able to deliver its promises, and how the new structures will be able to please more people for more of the time. It is more likely that television's responsiveness to viewers will be framed solely in marketing terms. To an increasing extent, it will be the interests of advertisers, not viewers, that television will have to serve.

Source

Tana Wollen and Janet Willis (eds) (1990) *The Broadcasting Debate: The Neglected Audience*, British Film Institute, pp. 1–2.

Questions

1. Why may public culture in the future be differentiated between the 'information-rich' and the 'information-poor'?
2. In what sense can a new concept of the audience as a collection of individuals be seen as detrimental?
3. Should the new technology be controlled and operated by 'private realms of ownership'? Are there viable alternatives?

General Questions

1. What determines the development of new technology and the ways in which it is used?
2. Market-orientated broadcasting policies are said to put consumer interests first and foremost. Why are so many commentators sceptical about this?

3. What arguments are there against regarding broadcasting solely as an industrial or commercial enterprise?
4. In what ways does new technology make issues of ownership and control central to any understanding of contemporary media?

Further Reading

Because new technology and its influence on national and international media policy is subject to almost weekly change, the most up-to-date comments are to be found in the media pages of papers such as *The Guardian*, and *The Independent*. Industry-orientated trade papers such as *Broadcast* and *Television Week* are also excellent source material. The following books are also very useful.

The six volumes in the series *The Broadcasting Debate*, published by the British Film Institute, are both readable and informative. They are, in volume order:

R. Paterson (ed.) (1990) *Organizing For Change*, Vol. 1.

G. Nowell-Smith (ed.) (1989) *The European Experience*, Vol. 2.

W. Stevenson and N. Smedley (eds) (1989) *Responses to the White Paper*, Vol. 3.

S. Bryant (ed.) (1989) *The Television Heritage*, Vol. 4.

T. Wollen and J. Willis (eds) (1990) *The Neglected Audience*, Vol. 5.

G. Mulgan (ed.) (1990) *The Question Of Quality*, Vol. 6.

In addition, the following books are recommended:

K. Dyson and P. Humphreys (eds) (1989) *Broadcasting and The New Media Technologies*, Routledge.

P. Lewis and J. Booth (1989) *The Invisible Medium*, Methuen.

R. Negrine (ed.) (1988) *Satellite Broadcasting: The Politics and Implications of The New Media*, Routledge.

C. Veljanovski (1988) *Freedom In Broadcasting*, Institute of Economic Affairs.

G. Wade (1986) *Film, Video and Television*, Comedia.

Index

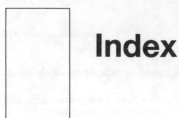